The Suppressed Truth

About the Assassination of Abraham Lincoln

Available Now On Amazon.com

Amazon.com/Suppressed-Truth-Assassination-Abraham-Lincoln/
dp/0996767711

Burke McCarty's brave and revealing 1922 expose of the Jesuits and their European and American conspirators who planned and carried out the assassination of iconic American President Abraham Lincoln.

Edited by William Dean A. Garner
New York Times bestselling ghostwriter/editor

Machiavelli's *The Prince*

Available Now On Amazon.com

Amazon.com/Prince-Niccolo-Machiavelli/dp/0996767703

The Prince isn't just for princes who thirst for, or are forcibly thrown into, advancement. It is a raw and bloody field manual for upper- and mid-level managers on predatorial ethics and power: what it is, how to obtain it, and what to do with it once you have found, stumbled across, or been granted it.

Edited by William Dean A. Garner
New York Times bestselling ghostwriter/editor

"What our enemies do not kill, the VA does. What our laws protect, the VA attacks. What God has given us in good health, the VA takes and destroys."

—Afghan & Iraq War Veteran

VA DISABILITY CLAIM

How to Prepare, File and Maintain a VA Disability Claim and Appeal

Jon Macintosh

adagio

adagio

AN INDEPENDENT PUBLISHING CRUISE
est. January 1, 2001

Katharine L. Petersen
Publisher / Senior Editor
William Dean A. Garner
Editor

Published in America by Adagio Press

Adagio and colophon are Trademarks of Adagio Press

Library of Congress Control Number: 2015957539

ISBN: 978-0-9967677-2-9

Adagio website: AdagioPress.com
Email: 69@adagiopress.com

Cover design: Dean Garner

B20161126
Third Print Edition

for All Disabled and Homeless Veterans
You have paid great sacrifices in war and training,
and come home to pay even further, some until death

and for You, dear Reader

INTRODUCTION

Since the release of the first edition of *VA Disability Claim*, I have received hundreds of emails and calls, plus read dozens of comments in different forums, from veterans, expressing praise and condemnation for the contents of my book.

These comments, sometimes bordering on outright threats, prompted me to reconsider the content of the next version of the book, because I wanted all veterans to feel they learned a lot from the materials I provided and got their money's worth.

Some veterans complained that I bashed the VA too much. Only a page or two would have sufficed, one said.

Others said they only wanted intel on how to prepare, file and maintain a VA disability claim.

Some of the old vets screamed at me for producing a "tiny book" they could barely read because of bad eyes, even though it looked "cool."

"Make a large-type version!" one vet wrote.

I hear you all, and thank you for taking the time to reach out to me and share your thoughts.

This is for all of you: I hereby respond by revamping my popular field manual.

The second edition features only intel on how to prepare, file and maintain a VA disability claim, plus helpful resources for those intrepid warriors who like to do research on their own. I have deleted all intel on the VA's misdeeds and malpractice issues, which you can still read in the first edition.

I did, however, retain the intel on veterans service organizations, because I felt it important that you know and understand how these people actually operate.

VA Disability Claim, first edition, has continued to be a bestselling book on Amazon, regularly ranking #1 in several different categories of Law (Military, Personal Injury and Disability), and selling many thousands of copies.

My hope with this new second edition is that it continues to inspire and assist veterans and their families with the many complex steps you must take to prepare, file and maintain a VA disability claim.

I invite all of you to visit my website/blog at VADisabilityClaimBook.com. Here I add helpful articles about the VA disability claim process, plus keep you up to date on various VA issues important to you, especially new VA programs like CHOICE.

As always, I welcome your feedback on all issues.

I wish you well on your journey. Whatever happens, do not quit! Only those who persevere to the sweet end are rewarded with a just VA disability award.

Jon Macintosh
Key West, Florida USA

1

THE PURPOSE OF THIS BOOK

What This Field Manual is Not About

VA Disability Claim does not cover information about vocational rehabilitation, employment, education, relocation, or benefits other than service-connected.

This book does not include the complex Integrated Physical Disability Evaluation System, which deserves a book of its own. Since it is a pilot program, there will be many changes in the next few years, making it challenging to write an accurate field manual on the subject.

VA Disability Claim is not a book on conspiracies, although some chapters discuss how the VA conspires against you and all veterans to deprive you of good healthcare and compensation for your injuries. It also provides steps you can take to possibly avoid or even counter these immoral and sometimes unlawful VA practices. It does not matter whether you believe these statements, because these terrible practices are going on as we speak and they will continue into the future, as long as we veterans and all good Americans allow them. The only thing you can do is withdraw from the VA healthcare system altogether . . . or learn how to manipulate it to your advantage. After all, the VA manipulates you every step of the way . . . to its own advantage, not yours.

VA Disability Claim is not about how to get the VA to acknowledge that your injuries are in fact service-connected. This is also a complex and involved process that surely deserves its own book or fold manual. See attorney Chris Attig's book on service-connection issues in the *References* section.

This field manual is not a long, drawn-out, negative account of how veterans are mistreated and lied to by the VA, or how the VA falsifies records and fabricates evidence on exam results. However, some chapters and sections do alert servicemembers and veterans about VA malfeasance and malpractice, and how to possibly avoid them or falling victim to the VA's oft-shoddy service.

VA Disability Claim is not a perfect, sure-fire method to get you, say, a 100% disability rating from the VA, or any other rating or award.

This field manual offers no guarantees whatsoever, even if you do all the steps diligently, simply because . . . shit happens regardless of how good you are and how well you perform at any given time and place.

What This Field Manual Can Do For You

VA Disability Claim has direct steps you can take to file your disability claim, but it is by no means perfect for all servicemembers and veterans. I have detailed the necessary steps for the average claim. Some claims will be more complicated and, therefore, no one book could possibly cover every aspect of the claims and appeals process. However, *VA Disability Claim* makes every effort to include everything you need to get started, plus a list of resources to consult for further information. I also state on many a page that you should consult a VA-accredited attorney at the earliest possible moment, so your rights are preserved and you do the right thing every step of the way.

This field manual is just like some of your favorite military field manuals: a short and simple quick-start guide of necessary steps to take to file, maintain and win your service-connected disability claim with the VA. It's like baking a Betty Crocker cake: simple step-by-step methods for you to use right away and get results, employing the most up-to-date procedures used and accepted by the VA and by law.

This manual was revised on 11 November 2015, following a flood of suggestions from readers of the first edition.

VA Disability Claim also pulls no punches when discussing the various negative parts of the claims process, how the VA and its representatives often conduct themselves unprofessionally and illegally, and how veterans service organizations work and do business on behalf of the VA and not the veteran.

This field manual will provide you with a good fighting chance to get what you are entitled to from the VA, help you maintain that rating, and increase it when necessary.

A suggestion: for those of you who wish to learn all about the VA claims and appeals process, please use this field manual along with John D. Roche's two outstanding books ***The Veteran's Survival Guide: How to File and Collect on VA Claims***, Second Edition and ***Claim Denied!*** Both books contain insider information about the VA claims process, although this knowledge is not necessary to file and win a VA disability claim.

They are now more than eight years old and, unfortunately, will never be updated due to his death in 2012. Many new laws, rules and regulations have come into effect since his books were published, some of which are discussed in ***VA Disability Claim***. Nonetheless, if you are interested in the in-depth process of how VA disability claims are handled by regional offices, please consult Mr. Roche's books. Both are listed in the *References* section at the end of this book and are currently available on Amazon.com.

I also strongly encourage you to purchase and read ***Navigating Legal Issues for Military Veterans: Leading Lawyers On Arguing Disability, Pension, and Other Claims Before the VA***, authored by seven different experts on the VA disability claims and appeals process. You will find it on Amazon.com for about $85, and it is worth every penny.

Curiously, ***Navigating Legal Issues for Military Veterans*** is not a guide designed for servicemembers or veterans. It was written for attorneys, but it is surprisingly readable and helpful. It is a wonderful resource for lawyers who wish to represent veterans in the VA disability appeals process, a handbook that tells it like it is. I suggest you purchase this book because, when used with this field manual, it will give servicemembers and veterans the best possible, easy-to-understand resources on the subject of VA disability claims and appeals for the layperson.

Please note that it is not necessary to learn all about the claims and appeals process before you prepare and file a VA disability claim. The additional information in ***Navigating Legal Issues for Military Veterans*** is valuable and may help those who are currently without legal representation.

As you read ***VA Disability Claim***, please form realistic expectations about the outcome of your own claim. Before you can do this, you must seek the expert advice of a good law firm or attorney who routinely handles disability cases against the VA.

Since all disappointments in life arise because of unexpressed communications and unfulfilled expectations, it is your duty and responsibility to ensure you have all the necessary information about your VA disability claim at your disposal, to provide you the best possible outcome with the least amount of money, effort, time and heartache.

Task, Conditions and Standards

Before you read this book, you must be prepared mentally for the first *task*, which is to prepare and file your VA disability claim. The *conditions* are the worst you are likely to find:

- VA healthcare workers who lie, falsify documents, and fabricate evidence on examinations.
- VA regional office officials who deny your claim outright, even if you prove your claim and provide all the necessary paperwork.

- Veterans service organizations' officers and employees who are ignorant of the law and thus provide you with unsatisfactory assistance.
- Board of Veterans Appeals judges and lawyers who ignore key evidence in your case and ultimately deny your claim.
- Court of Appeal for Veterans Claims judges who refuse to hear your case.

The *standards* are the highest: you must conduct yourself professionally and respectfully at all times, even in the face of reprehensible behavior by VA employees.

Given the task, conditions and standards, are you still interested in presenting your disability claim to the VA? Do you appreciate the fact that your case could take years before you receive a fair award? Are you prepared to put your family through mental hardship as a result of fighting the VA? Do you have the necessary resources to fight this monster? Are you prepared to do whatever it takes to win your case? If you are not sure, please watch the film, ***The Insider***, which details the uphill battle by Dr. Jeffrey Wigand, a whistleblower who took on BigTobacco in a most public way. The arduous journey is similar to those many of us have experienced. It is worth the two and a half hours of your hard-earned time.

If you answered no or even hesitated in your answers to the previous questions, then you need to do give this endeavor a long hard think, because the VA is prepared to mount an army of judges, lawyers, advisors, analysts, technicians and doodats who will do whatever it takes to win.

Will you? Most people quit near the end of anything, never knowing how close they came to reaching their goal.

You have survived a tour, if not an entire career, in the US military. Surely you can stand a little more heat and not simply survive but thrive during your VA disability claim or appeal fight. Recall what Sun Tzu said: "If you know the enemy and know yourself, you need not fear the result of a hundred battles."

How to Get What You Want

1. Set your goal.
2. Plan what it takes to attain it, using grit (determination and perseverance), then just do it.
3. Forget about the present, especially if it sucks for a long period of time. We humans overestimate how bad the present is and underestimate how much crap we can take.
4. Do not worry about or fear the future, because it's never as bad as you imagine it. We humans always overestimate how bad the future will be and usually end up quitting just before we reach the end.
5. Once you've thoroughly convinced yourself of items 3 and 4, and are on your way to doing whatever it takes to attain your goal, return to the present, the now, and revel in it throughout the entire journey.
6. Repeat 1-5 with your next goal.

Disclaimer and Author's Statement on Due Diligence

I am the sole author of this field manual: a former US military grunt with the 1st Ranger Battalion, 75th Ranger Regiment, now a veteran, who has gone through all steps of the VA claims process, except appeals to the US Supreme Court.

For this book, I have done my due diligence and listed only accurate, tried-and-true methods that get good, consistent results in favor of the veteran.

I have been in the VA Healthcare System for nearly 20 years, have successfully fought for and won a significant disability claim (60%), and have personally taken my cases and appeals to the highest levels of the VA claims process: the Board of Veterans Appeals and the Court of Appeals for Veterans Claims, and did so with and without the use of legal representation.

Also, I have employed several different veterans service organizations, all horribly ineffective, and also secured excellent legal representation (excellent!) that fought for and gained a significant increase in disability benefits and a change in the effective date of my initial claim. I've also gained additional secondary disability benefits that the VA had ignored for 15 years.

At the time of this critical update, 11 November 2015, any references, resources or internet links were the most up-to-date available. If you see that some resources have changed, please notify the publisher, 69@AdagioPress.com, or me (jon@vadisabilityclaimbook.com), as soon as possible so other veterans can be kept up to date with the latest and best information.

In short, I have conducted the best possible research using the best resources available at the time of production to write this field manual, and I stand behind my work fully. Also, my strong assessments of the VA, its healthcare system, and veterans service organizations are based on good, sound research and personal experiential experience, plus discussions and interviews with more than 2,000 veterans over nearly 20 years.

My supreme hope is that all servicemembers and veterans will receive strong, positive benefits from this field manual, and will pass on the knowledge and lessons learned to fellow servicemembers and veterans. The only way to beat the VA is to band together, learn the rules of this deadly game, apply those rules accurately and timely, and fight smartly.

So far, almost every single VA disability claim is fought as an epic David vs. Goliath battle that ends predictably: David loses. I hope and pray that we veterans will come together in the future and help each other so we all benefit, then pass what we have learned to the next generation of warriors and veterans.

Final Notes on *Why A Field Manual On Filing A VA Disability Claim?*:

1. **There is no one book on this subject that will give you all the information you need.** If your case is simple, then this book and those three I recommend will suffice. Just know that these books' authors have gone through thousands of books, manuals, documents, etc. to bring you the best possible intel on the subject of VA disability claims and appeals. And they've presented the results of their work in words that are easy to comprehend.

2. The VA is a giant monster that operates very inefficiently, yet no one wants to admit it. Very few members of Congress ever challenge the VA. And no one in the private sector gives a damn about the VA, although they laugh at how wasteful the VA is. You must learn how the VA operates so you can

best protect yourself during the entire claims and appeals process.

Read Senator Tom Coburn's recently published and highly detailed oversight report, *Friendly Fire: Death, Delay and Dismay at the VA.* It is a heartbreaking tale of woe at the VA, and will open your eyes to how poorly the VA actually operates, even though it advertises itself and its actions otherwise.

3. I have stated that my book was not designed to bash the VA, but I have spent time alerting servicemembers and veterans to the absolute facts about VA malfeasance and malpractice in the first edition of this book, still available on Amazon.com. I do so because I feel it is important for you to understand how the beast works, so you can best protect yourself and support your case.

4. This book was built as a field manual, with concrete steps you will take to prepare and file your claim and appeal. I had in mind my fellow special-operations grunts when I wrote this book: good, normal everyday men who were curious about the world and how things worked. The Q&A at the end of each chapter reflect some of their and others' queries about the whole claims and appeals process.

Q&A

I don't believe anything you've said about the VA being some corporation, so why should I bother reading this book?

Fair enough. Many people in this country do not believe that the US is really a corporation and its citizens are all slaves to it. It does sound a bit far-fetched, I admit.

Until you start doing in-depth research about who runs

the world and how they manage to do it. Then you'll discover that the US was actually designed and set up from the start to be an experimental corporation of docile workers, from whom the company would take much and give back little.

The VA is one of those companies designed in just this way, so it does not matter if you or anyone else believes this fact because it has been going on this way for more than 200 years, is happening as we speak, and will continue well into the future. Again, it does not matter what you think, because it's *real.*

If you choose to disregard the facts laid bare in this field manual, it is your choice. But I strongly suggest that you at least give it a fair shake and see how you do. I have proven these facts and methods to be accurate and effective.

Give this field manual a good go, follow through with all the steps and procedures, do what it takes to win your claim or appeal, and see what happens.

You said this book is for those who hate to read. Why is it so long then?

Every book on a complex subject requires some basic introduction to materials in each chapter, plus minimal background intel. I have strived to keep all chatter to an absolute minimum, while focusing only on those facts that are necessary for you to prepare, file, maintain, win and appeal a VA disability claim. In the end, I feel it was as short as I could make it.

You are a veteran who receives disability from the VA, yet you openly criticize the VA. Aren't you being hypocritical?

Not at all. My critical view about the VA is fair and accurate. In fact, it should be even more revealing, but this field manual is not about all the VA's shortcomings and illegal and immoral activities. It is important to point out some of the VA's bad behaviors, to give you an idea of the type of monster you are going into battle against. If you view the VA as a benevolent entity that acts in your best interest, then you will most likely lose your claim or case against the VA.

You mentioned two helpful books by John D. Roche, who was a VA claims examiner, and Navigating Legal Issues for Military Veterans, authored by seven different attorneys. Why these particular books?

Mr. Roche's books are excellent reads by a former insider who saw action at high levels of the claims process. His work is solid and his material is very helpful. Unfortunately, the two books are also out of date in some areas, as many new laws have come into effect since their publication.

Still, I recommend them as good background information about how claims examiners may view you and your claim, and how you may choose to act in light of this information.

The book by expert attorneys is a valuable resource that gives in-depth intel on the claims and appeals process. It is easy to read, has relevant stories about veterans and their experiences, and adds to your overall knowledge about the whole process of preparing and filing a claim or appeal.

Since I'm one who likes to do research and learn all I can, I found these books great resources that helped me understand the process better and also gave me a new appreciation for how attorneys work on behalf of veterans. When you understand and appreciate an attorney's role, you can better help him to help you in your case.

In the Task, Conditions and Standards, you make it sound impossible for a veteran to fight the VA. So why should I bother filing a claim?

It's not impossible. I state accurately what I've seen in hundreds of cases, heard or been involved in, or read about in case law and journal articles. I try to be as realistic as possible when documenting how the VA disability claims process works and how a veteran must perform to prevail in a case. Some people may see it as pessimistic or impossible.

My hope is that these people will get involved in their own claim and, with time, discover that it is not only possible to get through the whole process without going insane, they can actually win their disability award or case. It takes the same type of drive and determination, done over a long period of time, knowing in your heart, mind and soul that you can and will succeed.

Without this level of commitment, you will surely fail, and this is exactly what the VA wants you to do. I am sad to report that the vast majority of people do in fact fail because they gave up before they reached the end.

Here's a secret most don't know: from the veteran's perspective, the "end" of a case is when he or she wins. If you do not win, it is because you failed to take the necessary steps to win, or perhaps you did not have a good case to begin with.

After all, there are some veterans who file false claims and they get caught, which means their claims are denied.

So when I state that you can only win your case, I am assuming that you were in fact injured, your injury is service-connected, and you have the facts to back it up. The only possible outcome of your case is a win. All you have to do is see it through to the end. Of course, this does not mean that you will receive a 100% disability rating from the VA.

Let's be honest here: you only deserve what the law says is fair and accurate for your disability and nothing more, and you must be able to prove it. Just because the VA acts like a spoiled, rotten, psychopathic, abusive, and malevolent child does not mean you should, as well.

How can you openly criticize veterans service organizations, even though they are clearly America's darlings?

Veterans service organizations (VSOs) is a delicate subject I cover in that chapter, so please read it carefully. In general, veterans service organizations today are designed to appear to aid veterans and their families. And they do. Only in some areas.

But when it comes to the VA disability claims and appeals process, these veterans service organizations are clearly on the side of the hand that feeds them: the US Government and, hence, the VA.

One must carefully study the actions and behaviors of veterans service organizations to fully understand and appreciate how they work against the veteran during the claims and appeals process. Plus, their officers and representatives are not properly trained in the legal and medical fields, which are required to produce and present an excellent disability claim to the VA.

Again, the chapter, *Veterans Service Organizations*, goes into more depth on this subject and offers helpful advice on alternatives to using them.

To answer the above question directly, it is easy for me to openly challenge veterans service organizations, because they falsely advertise that they are veterans' advocates in the "adversarial" claims and appeals process, but in reality they are merely willing pawns of the VA, and their loyalty is not to you . . . it lies with the VA. I address this issue in an open letter to VA Secretary McDonald, which can be found on my website, VADisabilityClaimBook.com. I also address these issues in an open letter to President Obama. It can be found on my website.

2

PREPARE YOUR PAPERWORK

The valuable information in this field manual will save you years of time, effort, money and heartache, so read it, absorb its contents, become an expert in using its tools, and implement the lessons learned throughout your entire VA disability claim and case.

There is enough intel in this handy manual to guide you through the entire disability claims process on your own. There are also many helpful tips and bits of advice on how to seek outside assistance when needed.

Please do not do what I did: learn all about the VA claims process through many painful years of trial and error.

Why?

Because it took more than a dozen years to get it right, but I got to experience a lot in all phases of the disability claim process and that, in itself, was worth the time and effort and money spent.

I wrote this field manual so you would not have to go through all the pain and suffering I experienced. While I think it would be a great life lesson for you, something new to put in your bag of tricks, it is not necessary to become an expert in this whole process just to earn a fair and just disability award. If you are one of those folks who loves to learn something from inside out, then you will enjoy and get much satisfaction from this field manual and all the other books and resources I have listed at the end.

Learning how to represent yourself is not something I recommend to every veteran, simply because you must learn the law and that is a whole different profession that requires years of training and experience. You must become a legal expert in VA law and also become an expert at navigating the treacherous seas of the VA disability claims and appeals process. Neither are for the faint of heart.

If you are like the majority of military servicemembers and veterans, you want someone who has been through this entire process to show you the way, the shortest and most accurate route possible. And with the least amount of time, effort, money and pain.

Please read this field manual thoroughly and learn everything necessary so you can successfully file your disability claim. Each part of the claims process has concrete steps to take, and are listed in their logical order.

The various service branches have transition teams to assist you with the VA claims process, but please do not rely solely on them for advice and direction, because they are not experts and cannot give legal advice. They can, however, get you started, but you must be armed with prior knowledge of the whole VA claims process before you start asking questions or requesting assistance with your VA claim.

Document Everything

This is THE most important item to remember, especially if you are still on active duty.

If you are injured on the job, especially psychologically or sexually, see a healthcare provider immediately. Have them document the issues and injuries and note that they are service-connected, i.e. occurred on the job during your time in the military and were not the result of an issue that occurred prior to your service in the military. This step alone will save you a lot of time and effort, as it can be difficult once you enter the VA system to get a doctor to certify that your injuries or issues are service-connected.

For each issue or injury, ensure the accurate date/time stamp is noted and also exactly what events occurred before, during and after the issue or injury, what type of medical attention was sought and given, and the result, e.g. x ray, MRI, cast put on leg, rehab for a week, psychological or psychiatric counseling, etc. The more accurate you are in documenting your injuries and issues while you are still serving on active duty or in the reserves, the easier it will be for you when you are discharged and enter the VA system.

Not properly documenting injuries and issues is the number one mistake servicemembers make before being discharged.

They think that it won't matter later on and get lazy about

documenting medical problems. This is understandable, given all the stress associated with one's job in the military.

You must look at it this way: another important job of yours, which is just as important as your normal service job, is documenting all your medical injuries and issues and ensuring you have accurate paper and electronic records that are legible, plus a 100% accurate copy of these records, stored at a different location.

You must treat your personal medical records like a precious metal. And if you do not believe or appreciate this importance now, then please have your spouse or parents read this book so they can look after you and do the right thing on your behalf.

As a member of the US military, you are taught to suck it up and drive on, and not be a "weak" man or woman by complaining of any injuries or problems. On the battlefield, this is important for survival. But you also must be mentally and physically healthy to be an effective warrior, so when you're hurt, see someone and have them document the issue or injury as much as possible, and keep a record of it.

It may seem a pain to document every little detail, but you'll be grateful when you're separated from the military and are seeking VA disability benefits. Believe it or not, the devil is in the details, and the VA will use the details against you at every turn, so be prepared with the best possible information and case about your mental and physical health.

Do not suck it up and ignore your injury. It may get worse in the future and you will regret not having dealt with it properly when it happened by seeking medical assistance and getting copies of all the reports and exam results.

The number one complaint by recent veterans filing a disability claim and/or appeal: not having proper documentation of their injuries while in service.

I've said this already and it bears repeating because it's the reason why most veterans are denied disability awards for service-connected injuries. The most important point before you transition out of the military: get all your injuries noted by military doctors, and ensure military healthcare providers note that your injuries and disabilities are all service-connected and not due to issues, conditions and problems prior to your military service.

Keep the originals of all your military service records, esp. medical records, no matter how seemingly insignificant, including x-rays and all other films (MRIs, CT scans, etc.).

Every time you go to a medic, technician, nurse or physician, get a copy of the notes from the exam, take your own notes about what happened during the exam, and keep an accurate and well-organized set of records of everything related to your time in service and health. How many times have I stated this information so far? It is certainly not to annoy you to the point you stop reading this field manual.

This is especially true when you get any medical care through the VA CHOICE Program, where you see a non-VA physician for medical issues. The paperwork involved creates another layer of bureaucracy that will only get worse if you do not keep accurate copies of every procedure done and all doctor's notes, plus copies of all films from x-rays, MRIs, PET scans, etc.

Because CHOICE is so new, most veterans' representatives

do not know all the laws and rules governing the program. Again, keep copies of everything having to do with your CHOICE Program visits, tests, surgeries, etc.

I say again: the number one complaint by recent veterans filing a disability claim and/or appeal is not having proper documentation of their injuries while in service.

Be Careful What You Say

When talking to any medic, technician, nurse or physician, always be careful what you say because they will document it and the VA may use it against you at a later time.

Example: if you break your leg, do not tell a medic, technician, nurse or physician that you're fine and have no pain and can do your job well again. If you break your leg and say you're fine and can do all things normally again, when you apply for disability benefits in the future, the VA will use those old statements against you and deny your claim outright.

Be smart and keep some things to yourself. Previously I stated that you must document all injuries and issues while in the military, but you also must be smart here: think about how your statements to medical personnel might be interpreted. Again, if medical personnel hear from you that you are fine, not in any pain, and can return to duty without problems, then those medical personnel have just shot down your future case for a disability claim.

The legally smart thing to do in the case above is to get treated properly for the injury, have it properly documented by medical personnel, not state anything that can be used against you in the future, then get a copy of those records and exam results for future use. The less you say then, the more you win later on.

Doctor-Patient Confidentiality Is Not Confidential

Do not trust any medic, technician, nurse or physician with your deep thoughts and feelings, especially about your health and medical condition and mental health. Only state the actual injuries or symptoms, your level of pain and where it hurts and how often. Stick to the facts without divulging any statements that will sabotage your disability claim in the future.

Sadly, so-called "doctor-patient confidentiality" often works against patients, who are lured into the false notion that whatever they say cannot be disclosed to another person or entity. This is absolutely false. VA doctors, nurses and other employees are instructed to reveal personal and intimate details about patients, especially during claims evaluations and appeals, and they do all the time. Without the permission of the veteran.

This occurrence of sharing personal and "confidential" information is especially true if the patient (servicemember or veteran) states they are suicidal or intends to harm someone else or destroy property, or if they have already done harm. The VA healthcare workers are not obligated to inform the patient before that patient reveals information of this nature. The healthcare worker simply informs on the patient to proper authorities.

The Federal Rules of Evidence do not recognize "doctor-patient confidentiality," so the VA healthcare system workers are free to inform on its patients at any time for any reason, and this evidence is often used against veterans in claims and appeals.

Your Medical Records Are Your Life

Keep a copy of your entire service and medical records in a separate place outside your home, e.g. parents' home, safe deposit box, etc. When you go through the VA claims process, the VA will have its own copy of these records. It is most important that you always compare the VA's file it uses against you in all aspects of your claims case with the original file you have in your possession or safely stored off site. This means you will have two different and separate stacks of papers: one is a copy of what the VA has on file for you; the other is all the medical records you accumulated over the years you were in the military.

You must compare every single piece of paper in your collection of personal documents with what the VA has on file. If the VA has any documentation not in your file, then you must investigate what happened to your copies of those documents. In the least, you must make a copy of the VA's copy and place it in your own records, and make a note of this. In some cases, the VA has secured some documentation on veterans from outside sources. In the end, you then will have an accurate set of records on your medical injuries, issues, conditions, etc., which the VA also has.

The Battle Begins

Both you and the VA are now starting an epic battle with the same paperwork. Now all you need to do is make it work for you and not allow the VA to make it work against you.

Final Notes on *Prepare Your Paperwork*:

1. You absolutely must document everything about your medical history while in service, or it will come back to harm you when you are in the VA system.

2. Never assume that you can "get things straightened out when you ETS or retire." The VA system is designed to work against you, so do not count on it to have your complete medical records, let alone an accurate account of them.

3. If you think your VA physician is on your side, think again. This person works for the VA, is paid by the VA, and is loyal to the VA. When push comes to shove, your physician will not support you or your claim, because it is always in his best interest not to. Plus, he is given strict instructions by the VA not to render assistance beyond a certain level. Always look out for yourself and your healthcare, study the injuries and issues you suffer from, know what treatments are available, and understand the nature of any medications you take. The better armed you are with knowledge about your healthcare, the better you can defend yourself in the VA system.

Q&A

How do I get a copy of my service record?

First, only the following can request your service record:

- A military veteran, or
- Next of kin of a deceased, former member of the military. The next of kin can be any of the following:

  Surviving spouse that has not remarried
  Father

Mother
Son
Daughter
Sister
Brother

Go online to the National Archives's National Personnel Record Center: http://www.archives.gov/veterans/military-service-records/. You can make an online request for your service and medical records, but you need the following information on hand before you begin:

- The veteran's complete name used while in service
- Service number
- Social security number
- Branch of service
- Dates of service
- Date and place of birth (especially if the service number is not known).
- If you suspect your records may have been involved in the 1973 fire, also include:
- Place of discharge
- Last unit of assignment
- Place of entry into the service, if known.
- All requests must be signed and dated by the veteran or next-of-kin.
- If you are the next of kin of a deceased veteran, you must provide proof of death of the veteran such as a copy of death certificate, letter from funeral home, or published obituary.
- The purpose or reason for your request, such as applying for veterans benefits, preparing to retire,

or researching your personal military history.
- Any deadlines related to your request. Any other specificinformation,documentsorrecordsyourequire from your Official Military Personnel File (OMPF) besides your Report of Separation (DD Form 214).

How do I get a copy of my medical records?

Please contact the VA Records Management Center (VARMC) in St. Louis, MO: 888.533.4558. If a VA claim has been filed, they will send your medical records to the VA regional office that services your area. Contact the VARMC first to see where your medical records currently reside, then follow up with your VA regional office.

What is a C-file and how do I get a copy of it?

Your C-file is not simply your service and medical records. It is the complete (well, in theory, at least) set of documents the VA has on file for your claim and appeal. The VA uses all this information when studying and deciding your claim and appeal. Specifically, it has your complete service record, military medical records, VA medical records, plus correspondence and completed forms between you and the VA in your case.

That's why it is so important that you compare all your service and medical records you have compiled over the years to the C-file the VA has. The VA will use the information in your C-file in your claim and appeal.

You can request your C-file from your VA Regional Office by writing to the Freedom of Information Act (FOIA)/ Privacy Officer at the regional office. It is important that you use the FOIA request, because by law the VA must send it to you within 20 days. Send your FOIA request via certified mail, return receipt requested.

If you do not receive it within 20 days, then call your regional VA General Counsel. The office for your region can be found here: http://www.va.gov/ogc/rcoffices.asp. Send or fax another FOIA request to the office near you. They should send the C-file within 20 days.

If you do not receive your C-file within 20 days, call the VA Office of General Counsel in Washington, DC: (202) 273-6660. You should state that you have filed an FOIA request with no response and that you wish to have your complete and accurate C-file.

Beyond these extraordinary measures, you also can call your Congressman for assistance. Ask to speak with his FOIA officer and then fill him in on the details of your request. This is not the time to file a complaint against the VA because of its lack of assistance. Simply ask the FOIA officer to have your C-file sent to you.

As a last resort, you also can file a complaint in the nearest US federal district court, but you should ask your VA-accredited attorney for assistance.

If you do not use the above method, it will probably take about 6-9 months for you to receive your C-file.

The following ebook by attorney Chris Attig is very helpful with this entire process: *Take Back The Power: How to Get Your VA C-File. How To Get Your VA C&P Exam.*

I highly recommend purchasing all five of his books and using them along with this field manual.

3

FILE YOUR PREDISCHARGE CLAIM

For Active-Duty Servicemembers

WARNING: this and subsequent chapters contain highly detailed information, so please read everything carefully and follow the steps accordingly.

These are steps you will take to fill out a predischarge claim. They are clearly labeled STEP 1, STEP 2, etc. Each step is accurate, brief and concise, and has been vetted for 100% accuracy as of Veterans Day 2015.

Within 180 days before you are discharged, file a predischarge disability claim and request formal mental health and medical exams by a military physician, and ensure they do an accurate exam and assessment of all your issues and conditions.

Within about one week following the exam, get a copy of the complete exam notes, sometimes called Doctor's Notes, and read them carefully, noting any discrepancies, errors, and outright false statements and fabrications.

If you find anything inaccurate, talk with your first sergeant (or other NCOIC or OIC) and commanding officer about the problems, and request a new mental health and/or physical exam.

If your chain of command refuses to cooperate with you, see the next person up in your chain of command, and request a new mental health and/or physical exam. Explain where the physician erred in their exam results and be prepared to argue how they were incorrect or inaccurate.

If you're afraid to confront officers when one of their own has erred, especially when it concerns you and your life, then you're in for a long, hard life of disappointment.

Your chain of command is designed to get a job done, and when you upset it with medical issues, members of that chain will see you as a problem child, so tread carefully. Of course, you are leaving the military behind, so you may choose not to be so delicate when you argue your case.

You may in fact get a favorable and accurate disability rating when you leave service, based on the results of the predischarge exam, and will not have to endure years of fighting the VA. Sounds great on paper, but this is usually not the norm.

Please view the VA's YouTube video, *Step-by-Step Filing of an Electronic Fully Developed Claim (FDC)*: https://www.youtube.com/watch?v=RSzX029_ohA. Please note that the VA strongly advocates using a Veterans Service Organization.

In Step Two of the video, the VA shows a screenshot of the various choices you have for possible representation: Recognized Veterans Service Organization, Attorney, and

Claims Agent. The entire video is an advertisement for veterans using a Veterans Service Organization throughout the claim-filing process.

Curiously, the video does not mention, let alone strongly advocate, using a VA-accredited attorney to help you file your claim for VA disability. You must ask yourself *why* to fully understand the VA's underlying reasons.

For now, know that this is all by design: the VA secretly controls the US government's federally chartered Veterans Service Organizations, so it wants you to have them represent you and help you file your claim. Why? Because the chances of your being awarded the highest disability rating possible is not likely if you file on your own or use a Veterans Service Organization. This book's chapter, *Veterans Service Organizations*, explains the cozy relationship between the VA and Veterans Service Organizations. Please note that Veterans Service Organizations are not on your side, although they and the VA advertise them to be.

There are two types of predischarge claims available to active-duty servicemembers:

Benefits Delivery at Discharge (BDD)

Quick Start Claim (QSC)

Those serving overseas can apply for BDD or QSC through Overseas Intake Sites in Germany and Korea.

How To File A Benefits Delivery At Discharge Claim (BDD)

BDD is the fastest and most efficient way to file a predischarge claim. You can submit a claim for disability compensation 60 to 180 days before separation, retirement, or release from active duty or demobilization. The VA claims that you can receive benefits within 60 days after release or discharge, but this has been shown to be quite inaccurate. Many veterans report waits up to a year.

It is best if you file closer to 180 days before departure, because the BDD process needs a minimum of 60 days to allow sufficient time for the medical exams. If you cannot file a BDD near the 180-day mark and are less than 60 days from separation, you can submit a QSC. As of August 2014, BDD was available across the US and open to all full-time active duty servicemembers, including National Guard, Reserve and Coast Guard.

Additional requirements:

- You must have a known separation date before applying for BDD.
- You must apply within 180 to 60 days before separation.
- You must submit your complete service treatment records to the VA when filing the BDD application.
- You must complete all phases of the VA and DoD medical separation exam process before separation from military.

There are three different methods you can choose from to submit your claim:

1. Access forms and fill them out online; print them and send hard copies of complete package to your VA Regional Office.

2. Do the entire submission process online.
3. Start with hard-copy forms, fill them out by hand, submit complete package to your VA Regional Office.

The following is the first method: how to access forms at the eBenefits website, fill out the PDF forms online (i.e. not by hand), download and print them from your home computer, and submit the complete package to your VA Regional Office.

STEP 1

Set up an account at eBenefits: https://www.ebenefits.va.gov/ebenefits-portal/ebenefits.portal. This will allow you to access many of your VA records online at any time, fill out forms online, and also check the status of ongoing applications for benefits. The VA also has a good video of the steps you need to take, to get a DoD Self-Service (DS) Logon set up your eBenefits account: https://www.youtube.com/watch?v=QojXqc_TwUk

STEP 2

Once you have your new eBenefits account and DS Logon, search the eBenefits website for VA Form 21-526C (Pre-Discharge Compensation Claim), fill it out online, double-check your work, print two copies of the completed form.

A version of the form you can fill out online is here: http://www.vba.va.gov/pubs/forms/VBA-21-526c-ARE.pdf. I recommend filling it out online, saving the file to your desktop on your computer or laptop, and then printing the completed form. Ensure you make two copies, one to submit to the VA Regional Office near you and one for your personal records.

If you do not have access to a computer, ask someone in your chain of command for assistance in downloading the form.

STEP 3

By this step, you now have a completed VA Form 21-526C, which you have double-checked for accuracy. Ensure that you have not made any errors and that the form contains only the required information.

Take a complete copy of your service treatment records and place the completed form VA Form 21-526C on top. You never know how it will be handled, so I suggest placing the entire document inside a large ziploc bag, then place it inside a padded mailing envelope. If you can afford to send it via Next Day FedEx or UPS, do it. If not, you should send it US Postal Service Priority Mail with Certified Return Receipt via mail and email. If the return receipt is lost in the mail system, you should have a copy via email.

To find which VA Regional Office to send the package to, see http://www2.va.gov/directory/guide/map_flsh.asp. Click on your state, which takes you to a new VA page for that state, then do a search for "Regional Benefit Office," and click on the link for the office closest to you. For some states, there is only one office. For California, there are three.

On the right side of the page, you will find the name of the Regional Office and its mailing address. Use this address to mail your complete document.

The following is the second method: how to do the entire submission process online without downloading and printing the forms, and without physically mailing them:

STEP 1

As before, set up an account at eBenefits: https://www.ebenefits.va.gov/ebenefits-portal/ebenefits.portal. This will allow you to access many of your VA records online at any time, fill out forms online, and also check the status of ongoing applications for benefits. You also can view the VA's YouTube video that outlines nine steps to follow, to complete your claim application.

Even though this video is for a Fully Developed Claim and regular claim, you can follow the instructions and complete your application for a predischarge claim. The video is here: https://www.youtube.com/watch?v=RSzX029_ohA&feature=youtu.be

Always remember to save your work as often as possible. There is a button, SAVE & CONTINUE. Use it often in case your computer crashes or there is a power outage. Don't scoff at this, as it happens all the time and when you least expect it.

STEP 2

At the top of the page there is a row of links (Home, About, Help, etc.). Under these links, there is a row of tabs (Apply For Benefits, View My Status, etc.) Click on the first one: "Apply For Benefits," then under the heading Compensation click on "Apply For Disability Compensation."

You must read the Privacy Act Statement and click the

check box at the bottom to acknowledge and continue.

If you already have a VA File Number, enter it now. When the VA sends you written correspondence, it shows your VA File Number at the top of the fist page. It is almost always your social security number. If you do not have a VA File Number, click on the box labeled "I do not have a VA File Number," then click on SAVE & CONTINUE.

The next page is "Personal Information." Fill it out accurately and then double-check your work. It's important that you also have accurate banking information listed. It may already be listed, because the DoD carried it over from your direct deposit information while you were on active duty. Click SAVE & CONTINUE.

The next page is "Claim Notification," which states that you must complete the application within one year from starting it to preserve this claim and its "effective date." The VA will use the effective date of claim when paying you retroactive benefits.

You should fill out your application all at once, so be prepared with all your paperwork and documents. Click on the little box, "I understand these terms and conditions."

Then click SAVE & CONTINUE.

The next page is "Getting Started." Here you begin entering in information about your claim. You must have the following information on hand to complete it:

Service Information

- Branch of service
- Dates of service
- Duty status
- Date of separation from service

- Periods of confinement

Military Pay Information

- Type of post-discharge military pay
- Monthly amount receiving

Disability Records

- Disabilities and special issues

Treatment Records

- Dates of treatment
- Name of VA treatment center

Direct Deposit Information

- Account number
- Routing number

If there are any errors, you must correct them online. If your service dates are incorrect, you cannot correct them on this website. You must have proof of your dates of service, i.e. from your DD-214, and take this to your VA Regional Office and request to have your VA record corrected to reflect the accurate dates of service.

Click SAVE & CONTINUE.

You then will select the type of claim you are filing:

Original Disability Claim: this is the first time you have ever filed for VA compensation.

New Disability Claim: a new claim for a service-connected disability that has not been previously filed. You must add new disability information by clicking on the button, "Claim a New Disability," then add the appropriate information about this disability.

Reopened Disability Claim: reopening a previous disability claim that the VA disallowed. You can file this only after one year has passed since the VA disallowed the claim. Furthermore, you also must have new material evidence that supports reopening this claim.

Increased Disability Claim: you are asking the VA to evaluate an existing service-connected disability because it has increased in severity.

Secondary Disability Claim: select this if you have new problems or issues that resulted from an existing service-connected disability.

Once you have chosen which type of claim to file, click SAVE & CONTINUE.

On the "Confirm Treatment" page, you must indicate whether you have received medical treatment at any VA medical facility. At this point, you must have all relevant medical records ready to upload electronically.

Click SAVE & CONTINUE.

You have the option of asking the VA to assist you in locating any medical records by filing VA Form 21-4142. You should not need to do this if you have been diligent in gathering all your medical records on your own. Asking the VA to assist you at this point will greatly slow down the application process, probably by many months.

In addition to any private treatment records you may have, you can submit Disability Benefits Questionnaires (DBQ), which allow actively practicing, non-VA physicians to examine and diagnose you, then complete the appropriate DBQ. You may have multiple DBQs.

Before you upload your documents, ensure the electronic files are in an acceptable format: jpg, jpeg, tiff, gif, bmp, txt or unlocked pdf. No one file can exceed 5 MB (mega*bytes*, not megabits) in size. If you violate these rules, your work online may freeze or return error messages, so make sure you have the correctly formatted electronic documents before you begin the online application process and ensure each file is less than 5 MB.

On the "Documents to Include with Your Application" page, you will upload all your records and supporting documents. These may include DBQs, treatment notes, hospital records, outpatient records, and personal statements from family, friends and colleagues about your service-connected problems and issues.

Click on ADD or REMOVE FILES, then select the document type.

Click on BROWSE to locate the electronic files on your computer or external hard drive.

Then finally click on UPLOAD to begin uploading your document.

Repeat this process for each document you will be uploading in support of your application.

Click SAVE & CONTINUE.

Note: If you do not have access to a computer, ask someone in your chain of command for assistance in converting your records to Word or PDF documents and also in downloading the disability claim form.

If there are any errors, the "Error Check" page will display them. You must correct the errors before clicking on RECHECK.

Once your application is cleared, you will be taken to the "Final Validation" page where you will check to ensure that your application is 100% accurate. If anything is missing, you can click on one of the appropriate tabs at the top of the page, e.g. Disability Records or Direct Deposit, and correct it.

The final step is "Evidence Certification," where you verify that you have, in fact, enclosed all proper evidence, information, documents, etc. with your application. If there is nothing further to add, select "No More Evidence" and click on CONTINUE and then SUBMIT buttons.

The next page will issue you a confirmation number. Print the page for your records.

The third method is the easiest of all: get two or more copies of the claim form from the VA, or by downloading from the eBenefits website or VA site, fill them out by hand, and use the information in Step 3 above to submit the complete package to your VA Regional Office.

Regardless of which method you choose, once you complete the steps, you are done with the BDD application process. For now, finish out your time in service, stay healthy and happy, and then prepare yourself to deal with the VA.

How To File A Quick Start Claim (QSC)

The QSC filing process is the same for BDD, except that you are now filing a QSC instead of BDD, and will have to wait additional time to receive any benefits.

If you missed the last day to file a BDD, i.e. less than 60 days from separation from active duty, then you can file a QSC at 59 or fewer days before your separation, retirement, or release from active duty or demobilization date.

QSC is available across the US and open to all full-time active duty servicemembers, including members of the National Guard and Reserves. For Coast Guard members, please check with your transition team supervisor.

Additional requirements:

You must have a known separation date before applying for QSC.

You must apply within 59 days before separation.

You must submit your complete service treatment records to the VA when filing the QSC application.

You must complete all phases of the VA and DoD medical separation exam process before separation from military.

The methods and steps for submitting your QSC are the same as in the BDD process above.

Once you complete these three steps, you are done with the QSC application process. Since you missed the deadline to file for BDD, you now must wait longer to receive your benefits or, in the least, a decision on your claim.

How To File Via Overseas Intake Sites

If you are stationed in Europe, Africa or the Middle East, please contact the BDD Office in Landstuhl, Germany. You must file within 180 days of your separation or retirement date and be available to visit Landstuhl for physical or mental-health exams, or any other issue.

If you are stationed within the Kaiserslautern Military Community, you must submit your completed VA Form 21-526 and service treatment records to the Landstuhl BDD

Office in person. Please contact them for the most up-to-date hours of operation.

Servicemembers stationed outside the Kaiserslautern Military Community must use the "Fly-in" claim process, which allows servicemembers to submit applications by fax or e-mail. You will make only one trip to Landstuhl to complete a physical examination and submit your application.

Contact information:
BDD Office
Landstuhl Regional Medical Center
Bldg 3700 Room 214
Phone: DSN 486-8028 or CIV 06371-86-8028
(0049-6371-86-8028 outside Germany)
Fax: DSN 486-7886 or CIV 06371-86-7886
(0049-6371-86-7786 outside Germany)
Email: GermanyBDD.vbapit@va.gov

If you have questions about the predischarge claim process while you are still on active duty, please contact your Transition Assistance Office or ACAP Center (Army only). Your office can also schedule you to attend VA benefits seminars on filing your claim.

The VA suggests that you can also call the VA toll-free at 1-800-827-1000, but please corroborate any intel you get from the VA representative with this field manual, other resources listed in this manual, and any trusted advisor on your transition team.

Never trust a VA phone representative to give you accurate advice or instructions on how to file or fill out forms. Write down everything they tell you and always verify it with your attorney or representative. These VA phone representatives are not properly trained by the VA to dispense accurate information, but are trained to act like they know what they are talking about. Remember: always look after yourself.

Final Notes on *File Your Predischarge Claim*:

1. Have a complete copy of your service and medical records in both hard copy and electronic format.
2. Store your personal copy of your service records and service treatment record in a safe and secure place.
3. Learn to use a computer and the internet, so you can use both to file, maintain and track your disability claims applications online.
4. Follow the rules and deadlines, so you do not lose the opportunity to file and collect disability benefits.

Q&A

Can't I just wait to file a disability claim when I ETS or retire from the military?

Yes, but you will end up waiting six to 12 months for a decision. Why wait so long when it is possible that you could get a favorable disability rating upon exit? I strongly recommend that all servicemembers file their predischarge claim well within the required time, as specified in this chapter.

Realistically, what if there is no time for me to file a predischarge claim?

Talk with your OIC or NCOIC to figure out how you

can file a predischarge claim. If necessary, go up the chain of command until you find someone who will listen and make it happen. If necessary, ask for an extension to file, if possible. The worst that can happen is that you must wait until after your discharge or retirement to file your claim.

4

FILE YOUR DISABILITY CLAIM

For Veterans

On 24 September 2014, the VA announced that it would adopt new standard forms to streamline the claims and appeals process.

One of the most important is VA Form 21-0966, Intent To File A Claim For Compensation And/Or Pension, Survivors Pension, Or Other Benefits.

It is available as an automatic download from my site: VADisabilityClaimBook.com/21-0966(7-30-14).pdf.

The purpose of this form is to notify the VA of your intent to file for the general benefit(s) you describe. The form is very important because it preserves the *effective date* of your claim, even if you actually file your claim one year later.

For those eligible to receive retroactive benefits, this can mean an extra year of a retro awards, which may be substantial. Since this is such a simple and straightforward one-page form, I will not provide detailed instruction on how to fill it out. Just ensure you follow the directions accurately.

The VA also launched the new VA Form 21-526EZ for veterans to file for the following benefits:

- Fully Developed Claim
- Disability Service Connection
- Secondary Service Connection
- Increased Disability Compensation
- Temporary Total Disability Rating
- Individual Unemployability
- Compensation under 38 U.S.C. 1151
- Additional Special Monthly Compensation
- Specially Adapted Housing/Special Home Adaptation
- Automobile Allowance/Adaptive Equipment
- Benefits Based on a Veteran's Seriously Disabled Child

The VA stated, "Standardizing the process by which Veterans file claims and initiate appeals will make it easier for Veterans and their survivors to clearly state what benefits they are seeking from VA and provide information that is necessary to process their claims and appeals.

The new forms eliminate applicant guesswork, which often leads to delays in decisions and ultimately delays in receiving benefits. The new regulations go into effect in late March 2015."

Curiously, the VA placed 100% blame for "delays in decisions and ultimately delays in receiving benefits" on the veteran. . . .

Like the preceding chapter, *File Your Disability Claim* has concrete steps you will take to fill out either a Fully Developed Claim (FDC) or regular disability claim. They are clearly labeled STEP 1, STEP 2, etc. Each step is accurate, brief and concise, and has been vetted for 100% accuracy as of Veterans' Day, 11 November 2015.

However, the VA does make frequent changes to its programs and processes, especially the FDC, so please be patient if some part of the claims application process does not go smoothly.

Recall your SURVIVAL skills:

Size up the situation
Use all your senses
Remember where you are
Vanquish all fears
Improvise
Value life
Act like the natives
Live by your wits and good common sense

Once you calm down and find the updated information, you will be on your way to completing the task.

If you already filed a predischarge claim and received a favorable disability rating from the VA after your discharge, you should file for an increase in disability benefits or for injuries that were ignored or overlooked by the military and VA before, during and after separation.

You can also file at a later date, but the best time to file is the date you receive a rating from the VA, based on your predischarge or exit physical. That way your "effective date" of your VA disability claim will be preserved as early as possible, and you will be entitled to a larger retro payment when your VA claim is settled to your satisfaction. Do not wait too long to file or you may lose or postpone future benefits.

If you did not file a predischarge claim while on active

duty, there are two options: you can file an FDC or a regular disability claim. The FDC is a fast-tracked claim for those veterans who have already prepared their medical records and supporting evidence, and have an excellent case that proves their service-connected disability.

You must be on the ball here before even thinking about submitting this type of claim, because your entire case must already be outlined in detail, and you must have good, accurate medical records to back up your claim fully.

The best person to assist you in preparing this type of claim is an attorney experienced in VA disability claims. If you do not have one, the next best advisor is a veterans service organization officer who is well-versed in submitting FDCs. Don't be afraid to ask him if he's fluent in the process, or how many FDCs he's filed in the past.

It won't do much good to ask what the outcomes of those claims were, but try anyway. Some veterans service officers are helpful and forthcoming, and may give you some advice that assists you on other matters in the future.

How The VA Rates Veterans

A veteran's Range of Motion (ROM) is *the* most important criterion the VA uses when assigning a disability rating to a veteran, although the VA and its advocates will strenuously disagree. I discuss Range of Motion in a detailed article on my website: "A New Suggested Calculation For Range Of Motion (ROM) In VA C&P Exams."

For example, if you have a hip injury and, from a lying position on your back, can flex your leg only a certain number of degrees from the table, then during the exam do so and not one degree more. The examiner will use a measuring instrument called a goniometer to note the number of degrees of flexion. He also will use this instrument to measure the ROM of any affected limb(s), head and torso.

Unfortunately, approximately 85% of the hundreds of veterans surveyed stated that the C&P examiner did not use a goniometer during their C&P exam. And 100% of the same veterans stated that the examiner was inaccurate when measuring ROM.

Most veterans also stated that examiners did not perform some if not many of the exercises during the exam, and outright lied and falsified data on those exams. Worst of all, examiners in the majority of cases (more than 90%) fabricated evidence to show the veteran had normal ROM, which resulted in the VA denying disability benefits to more than 90% of those veterans.

The veteran's only recourse is to file VA Form 21-0958 (Notice of Disagreement, NOD) with the VA.

The veteran should file with the VA a brief letter that states the exam was an "inadequate examination" and outlines where the examiner erred or fabricated evidence.

In most cases, the VA will ignore this letter, but at least it becomes part of the veteran's case file and can be used in appeal or in court, if necessary, especially by a good law firm or attorney. However, the NOD formally commences the appeals process.

How To Conduct Yourself

If you have injuries to the limbs, then you must show the examiner that your ROM is poor. If you have painful motion that starts the moment you flex or extend the limb, then yell out! The examiner is supposed to note that the pain started at 0 or 5 degrees, and continued for the range of motion of that movement.

In general, **move as little as possible**, because the C&P examiner will lie about your ROM to make it look like your ROMs were normal, and your claim will be denied.

Be respectful and professional at all times. Do not try to intimidate the examiner, call him silly names or belittle him in any way, because he may call VA Police and have you escorted out of the facility or even arrested and charged with a crime.

Antagonizing the examiner will work against you in the future and you could possibly be denied further treatment at that facility because of your inappropriate behavior. Just because the examiner is acting badly or is obviously lying or fabricating evidence against you and your case does not give you cause to act anything less than respectful and professional at all times.

When a law firm or attorney takes your case, your good behavior will work in your favor or, in the least, not against you and your case.

How to File a Fully Developed Claim (FDC)

The procedures are like those for filing a Predischarge Claim, and you have the same three options:

1. Access VA Form 21-526EZ and fill it out online; print it and send hard copies of complete package to your VA Regional Office.
2. Do the entire submission process online.

3. Start with hard-copy a form, fill it out by hand, submit complete package to your VA Regional Office.

The following is the first method: how to access forms at the eBenefits website, fill out the PDF forms online (i.e. not by hand), download and print them from your home computer, and submit the complete package to your VA Regional Office.

STEP 1

Set up an account at eBenefits: https://www.ebenefits.va.gov/ebenefits-portal/ebenefits.portal. This will allow you to access many of your VA records online at any time, fill out forms online, and also check the status of ongoing applications for benefits. The VA also has a good video of the steps you need to take, to get a DoD Self-Service (DS) Logon set up your eBenefits account: https://www.youtube.com/watch?v=QojXqc_TwUk.

STEP 2

Once you have your new eBenefits account and DS Logon, search the eBenefits website for VA Form 21-526EZ, fill out the entire application online, double-check your work, print two copies of the completed form.

I recommend filling it out online, saving the file to your desktop on your computer or laptop, and then printing the completed form. Ensure you make two copies, one to submit to the VA Regional Office near you and one for your personal records.

If you do not have access to a computer, ask a friend or colleague for assistance in downloading and printing the form.

STEP 3

By this step, you now have a completed and double-checked the application for accuracy. Ensure that you have not made any errors and that the application contains only the required information.

Take a complete copy of your service treatment records and place the completed application on top. You never know how it will be handled, so I suggest placing the entire document inside a large ziploc bag, then place it inside a padded mailing envelope. If you can afford to send it via Next Day FedEx or UPS, do it. If not, you should send it US Postal Service Priority Mail with Certified Return Receipt via mail and email. If the return receipt is lost in the mail system, you should have a copy via email.

To find which VA Regional Office to send the package to, see http://www2.va.gov/directory/guide/map_flsh.asp. Click on your state, which takes you to a new VA page for that state, then do a search for "Regional Benefit Office," and click on the link for the office closest to you. For some states, there is only one office. For California, there are three.

On the right side of the page, you will find the name of the Regional Office and its mailing address. Use this address to mail your complete document.

The following is the second method: how to do the entire submission process online without downloading and printing VA Form 21-526EZ, and without physically mailing it. It is identical to the process in the previous chapter, but is printed here in its entirety for clarity:

STEP 1

As before, set up an account at eBenefits: https://www.ebenefits.va.gov/ebenefits-portal/ebenefits.portal. This will allow you to access many of your VA records online at any time, fill out forms online, and also check the status of ongoing applications for benefits.

You also can view the VA's YouTube video that outlines nine steps to follow, to complete your claim application. The video is here: https://www.youtube.com/watch?v=RSzX029_ohA

Always remember to save your work as often as possible. There is a button, SAVE & CONTINUE. Use it often in case your computer crashes or there is a power outage. Don't scoff at this, as it happens all the time and when you least expect it.

STEP 2

At the top of the page, there is a row of links (Home, About, Help, etc.). Under these links, there is a row of tabs (Apply For Benefits, View My Status, etc.) Click on the first one: "Apply For Benefits," then under the heading Compensation click on "Apply For Disability Compensation."

You must read the Privacy Act Statement and click the check box at the bottom to acknowledge and continue.

If you already have a VA File Number, enter it now. When the VA sends you written correspondence, it shows your VA File Number at the top of the fist page. It is almost always your social security number. If you do not have a VA File Number, click on the box labeled "I do not have a VA File Number," then click on SAVE & CONTINUE.

The next page is "Personal Information." Fill it out

accurately and then double-check you work. It's important that you also have accurate banking information listed. It may already be listed, because the DoD carried it over from your direct deposit information while you were on active duty. Click SAVE & CONTINUE.

The next page is "Claim Notification," which states that you must complete the application within one year from starting it to preserve this claim and its "effective date." The VA will use the effective date of claim when paying you retroactive benefits. You should fill out your application all at once, so be prepared with all your paperwork and documents. Click on the little box, "I understand these terms and conditions."

Then click SAVE & CONTINUE.

The next page is "Getting Started." Here you begin entering in information about your claim. You must have the following information on hand to complete it:

Service Information

- Branch of service
- Dates of service
- Duty status
- Date of separation from service
- Periods of confinement

Military Pay Information

- Type of post-discharge military pay
- Monthly amount receiving

Disability Records

- Disabilities and special issues

Treatment Records

- Dates of treatment
- Name of VA treatment center

Direct Deposit Information

- Account number
- Routing number

If there are any errors, you must correct them online. If your service dates are incorrect, you cannot correct them on this website. You must have proof of your dates of service, i.e. from your DD-214, and take this to your VA Regional Office and request to have your VA record corrected to reflect the accurate dates of service.

Click SAVE & CONTINUE.

You then will select the type of claim you are filing:

Original Disability Claim: this is the first time you have ever filed for VA compensation.

New Disability Claim: a new claim for a service-connected disability that has not been previously filed. You must add new disability information by clicking on the button, "Claim a New Disability," then add the appropriate information about this disability.

Reopened Disability Claim: reopening a previous disability claim that the VA disallowed. You can file this only after one year has passed since the VA disallowed the claim. Furthermore, you also must have new material evidence that supports reopening this claim.

Increased Disability Claim: you are asking the VA to evaluate an existing service-connected disability because it has increased in severity.

Secondary Disability Claim: select this is you have new problems or issues that resulted from an existing service-connected disability.

Once you have chosen which type of claim to file, click

SAVE & CONTINUE.

On the "Confirm Treatment" page, you must indicate whether you have received medical treatment at any VA medical facility. At this point, you must have all relevant medical records ready to upload electronically.

Click SAVE & CONTINUE.

You have the option of asking the VA to assist you in locating any medical records by filing VA Form 21-4142. You should not need to do this if you have been diligent in gathering all your medical records on your own. Asking the VA to assist you at this point will greatly slow down the application process, probably by many months.

In addition to any private treatment records you may have, you can submit Disability Benefits Questionnaires (DBQ), which allow actively practicing, non-VA physicians to examine and diagnose you, then complete the appropriate DBQ. You may have multiple DBQs.

Before you upload your documents, ensure the electronic files are in an acceptable format: jpg, jpeg, tiff, gif, bmp, txt or unlocked pdf. No one file can exceed 5 MB in size. If you violate these rules, your work online may freeze or return error messages, so make sure you have the correctly formatted electronic documents before you begin the online application process and ensure each file is less than 5 MB (again, this is 5 mega*bytes*).

On the "Documents to Include with Your Application" page, you will upload all your records and supporting documents. These may include DBQs, treatment notes, hospital records, outpatient records, and personal statements from family, friends and colleagues about your service-connected problems and issues.

Click on ADD or REMOVE FILES, then select the document type.

Click on BROWSE to locate the electronic files on your computer or external hard drive.

Then when you have completed the steps, click on UPLOAD to begin uploading your document.

Repeat this process for each document you will be uploading in support of your application.

Click SAVE & CONTINUE.

Note: If you do not have access to a computer, ask someone for assistance in converting your records to Word or PDF documents and also in downloading the disability claim form.

If there are any errors, the "Error Check" page will display them. You must correct the errors before clicking on RECHECK.

Once your application is cleared, you will be taken to the "Final Validation" page where you will check to ensure that your application is 100% accurate. If anything is missing, you can click on one of the appropriate tabs at the top of the page, e.g. Disability Records or Direct Deposit, and correct it.

The final step is "Evidence Certification," where you verify that you have, in fact, enclosed all proper evidence, information, documents, etc. with your application. If there is nothing further to add, select "No More Evidence" and click on CONTINUE and then SUBMIT buttons.

The next page will issue you a confirmation number. Print the page for your records.

The third method is the easiest of all: get two or more copies of VA Form 21-526EZ from the VA, or by downloading from the eBenefits website or VA site, fill it out by hand, and use the information in Step 3 above to submit the complete package to your VA Regional Office.

Regardless of which method you choose, once you complete the steps, you are done with the FDC application process. The only further steps you can take are to ensure the VA Regional Office received your complete application package and that it is now in review. After that, I suggest finding something worthwhile to occupy your time, because the VA claims process is excruciatingly slow and often ineffective.

Every few months, you may choose to contact your attorney or service organization representative and ask them for an update. The VA allows service organization representatives access to some of its files, so the reps can view the status of a claim or appeal. Alternatively, you can walk in the VA Regional Office and talk with a customer service representative about the status of your claim.

How To File A Regular Disability Claim

The procedures are almost identical to filing an FDC, and you have the same three options:

1. Access VA Form 21-526EZ and fill it out online; print it and send hard copies of complete package to your VA Regional Office.
2. Do the entire submission process online.
3. Start with a hard-copy form, fill it out by hand, submit complete package to your VA Regional Office.

The following is the first method: how to access VA Form 21-526EZ at the eBenefits website, fill out the PDF form online (i.e. not by hand), download and print it from your home computer, and submit the complete package to your VA Regional Office.

STEP 1

Set up an account at eBenefits as described in the previous chapter:

https://www.ebenefits.va.gov/ebenefits-portal/ebenefits.portal.

This will allow you to access many of your VA records online at any time, fill out forms online, and also check the status of ongoing applications for any type of benefit you may have applied for.

STEP 2

Search the eBenefits website for VA Form 21-526EZ, fill out the entire application online, double-check your work, print two copies of the completed form. I recommend filling it out online, saving the file to your desktop on your computer or laptop, and then printing the completed form. Ensure you make two copies, one to submit to the VA Regional Office near you and one for your personal records.

If you do not have access to a computer, ask a friend or colleague for assistance in downloading and printing the form.

STEP 3

By this step, you now have a completed and double-checked the application for accuracy. Ensure that you have not made any errors and that the application contains only the required information.

Take a complete copy of your service treatment records and place the completed application on top. You never know how it will be handled, so I suggest placing the entire document inside a large ziploc bag, then place it inside a padded mailing envelope. If you can afford to send it via Next Day FedEx or UPS, do it. If not, you should send it US Postal Service Priority Mail with Certified Return Receipt via mail and email. If the return receipt is lost in the mail system, you should have a copy via email.

To find which VA Regional Office to send the package to, see http://www2.va.gov/directory/guide/map_flsh.asp. Click on your state, which takes you to a new VA page for that state, then do a search for "Regional Benefit Office," and click on the link for the office closest to you. For some states, there is only one office. For California, there are three.

On the right side of the page, you will find the name of the Regional Office and its mailing address. Use this address to mail your complete document.

The following is the second method: how to do the entire submission process online without downloading and printing the forms, and without physically mailing them:

STEP 1

As before, set up an account at eBenefits: https://www.ebenefits.va.gov/ebenefits-portal/ebenefits.portal. This will allow you to access many of your VA records online at any time, fill out forms online, and also check the status of ongoing applications for benefits. You also can view the VA's YouTube video that outlines nine steps to follow, to complete your claim application. The video is here: https://www.youtube.com/watch?v=RSzX029_ohA&feature=youtu.be

Always remember to save your work as often as possible. There is a button, SAVE & CONTINUE. Use it often in case your computer crashes or there is a power outage. Don't scoff at this, as it happens all the time and when you least expect it.

STEP 2

At the top of the page there is a row of links (Home, About, Help, etc.). Under these links, there is a row of tabs (Apply For Benefits, View My Status, etc.) Click on the first one: "Apply For Benefits," then under the heading Compensation click on "Apply For Disability Compensation."

You must read the Privacy Act Statement and click the check box at the bottom to acknowledge and continue.

If you already have a VA File Number, enter it now. When the VA sends you written correspondence, it shows your VA File Number at the top of the first page. It is almost always your social security number. If you do not have a VA File Number, click on the box labeled "I do not have a VA File Number," then click on SAVE & CONTINUE.

The next page is Personal Information. Fill it out accurately and then double-check you work. It's important that you also have accurate banking information listed. It may already be listed, because the DoD carried it over from your direct deposit information while you were on active duty. Click Save and Continue.

The next page is "Claim Notification," which states that you must complete the application within one year from starting it to preserve this claim and its "effective date." The VA will use the effective date of claim when paying you retroactive benefits. You should fill out your application all at once, so be prepared with all your paperwork and documents. Click on the little box, "I understand these terms and conditions."

Then click SAVE & CONTINUE.

The next page is "Getting Started." Here you begin entering in information about your claim. You must have the following information on hand to complete it:

Service Information

- Branch of service
- Dates of service
- Duty status
- Date of separation from service
- Periods of confinement

Military Pay Information

- Type of post-discharge military pay
- Monthly amount receiving

Disability Records

- Disabilities and special issues

Treatment Records

- Dates of treatment
- Name of VA treatment center

Direct Deposit Information

- Account number
- Routing number

If there are any errors, you must correct them online. If your service dates are incorrect, you cannot correct them on this website. You must have proof of your dates of service, i.e. from your DD-214, and take this to your VA Regional Office and request to have your VA record corrected to reflect the accurate dates of service.

Click SAVE & CONTINUE.

You then will select the type of claim you are filing:

Original Disability Claim: this is the first time you have ever filed for VA compensation.

New Disability Claim: a new claim for a service-connected disability that has not been previously filed. You must add new disability information by clicking on the button, "Claim a New Disability," then add the appropriate information about this disability.

Reopened Disability Claim: reopening a previous disability claim that the VA disallowed. You can file this only after one year has passed since the VA disallowed the claim. Furthermore, you also must have new material evidence that supports reopening this claim.

Increased Disability Claim: you are asking the VA to evaluate an existing service-connected disability because it has increased in severity.

Secondary Disability Claim: select this if you have new problems or issues that resulted from an existing service-connected disability.

Once you have chosen which type of claim to file, click SAVE & CONTINUE.

On the "Confirm Treatment" page, you must indicate whether you have received medical treatment at any VA medical facility. At this point, you must have all relevant medical records ready to upload electronically.

Click SAVE & CONTINUE.

You have the option of asking the VA to assist you in locating any medical records by filing VA Form 21-4142. You should not need to do this if you have been diligent in gathering all your medical records on your own. Asking the VA to assist you at this point will greatly slow down the application process, probably by many months.

In addition to any private treatment records you may have, you can submit Disability Benefits Questionnaires (DBQ), which allow actively practicing, non-VA physicians to examine and diagnose you, then complete the appropriate DBQ. You may have multiple DBQs.

Before you upload your documents, ensure the electronic files are in an acceptable format: jpg, jpeg, tiff, gif, bmp, txt or unlocked pdf. No one file can exceed 5 MB in size. If you violate these rules, your work online may freeze or return error messages, so make sure you have the correctly formatted electronic documents before you begin the online application process and ensure each file is less than 5 MB.

On the "Documents to Include with Your Application" page, you will upload all your records and supporting documents. These may include DBQs, treatment notes, hospital records, outpatient records, and personal statements from family, friends and colleagues about your service-connected problems and issues.

Click on ADD or REMOVE FILES, then select the document type.

Click on BROWSE to locate the electronic files on your

computer or external hard drive.

Then finally click on UPLOAD to begin uploading your document.

Repeat this process for each document you will be uploading in support of your application.

Click SAVE & CONTINUE.

Note: If you do not have access to a computer, ask someone for assistance in converting your records to Word or PDF documents and also in downloading the disability claim form.

If there are any errors, the "Error Check" page will display them. You must correct the errors before clicking on RECHECK.

Once your application is cleared, you will be taken to the "Final Validation" page where you will check to ensure that your application is 100% accurate. If anything is missing, you can click on one of the appropriate tabs at the top of the page, e.g. Disability Records or Direct Deposit, and correct it.

The final step is "Evidence Certification," where you verify that you have, in fact, enclosed all proper evidence, information, documents, etc. with your application. If there is nothing further to add, select "No More Evidence" and click on CONTINUE and then SUBMIT buttons.

The next page will issue you a confirmation number. Print the page for your records.

The third method is the easiest of all: get two or more copies of VA Form 21-526EZ from the VA, or by downloading from the eBenefits website or VA site, fill it out by hand, and use the information in Step 3 above to submit the complete

package to your VA Regional Office.

The only further steps you can take are to ensure the VA Regional Office received your complete application package and that it is now in review. Every few months, contact your attorney or service organization representative and ask them for an update. The VA allows service organization representatives access to some of its files, so the reps can view the status of a claim or appeal. You also can walk directly into your VA Regional Office and request an update on the status of your claim.

Final Notes on *File Your Disability Claim*:

1. Have a complete copy of your service and medical records in both hard copy and electronic format.
2. Store your personal copy of your service records and service treatment record in a safe and secure place.
3. Learn to use a computer and the internet, so you can use both to file, maintain and track your disability claims applications online.
4. Follow the rules and deadlines, so you do not lose the opportunity to file and collect disability benefits.
5. Hire a VA-accredited attorney to assist you in preparing all your documents and forms. You may have to pay him for services rendered at this point, but it will be worth any cost and fees, which most likely will be less than $1,200 for a few hours' work.

The attorneys I spoke with normally will not take a case on contingency until the NOD is filed or they file it on your behalf, because, if they took the case on a contingency, the law forbids them from getting paid for these services until after the NOD has been filed.

6. Do not rely on a Veterans Service Organization (VSO) representative to assist you, because they are not well trained like a VA-accredited attorney. Please see the next chapter, Veteran Service Organizations, for detailed information.

Q&A

Why should I spend the money to hire a VA-accredited attorney when my Veterans Service Organization has guys who will help me for free?

Simply put, you get what you pay for. VSOs have many officers and representatives on staff to assist veterans on all levels. However, these VSO representatives are not well trained, they do not possess the legal or medical skills to adequately assist you in your claim, and each one represents hundreds or thousands of veterans, so they could not possibly spend the necessary time to assist you well.

Get a VA-accredited attorney to help you fill out all the necessary paperwork and forms, compile your documents into a good, sound file, and submit it to the VA. You will pay several hundred dollars, if not more, but the money will be well spent. If you do not have the money, save each month for a year before you ETS or retire. Ask your family members for support, but explain to them first what you are doing and how important it is to have an attorney assist you in the claims process. As a last resort, take out a loan to pay the attorney.

5

VETERANS SERVICE ORGANIZATIONS

This was a very difficult chapter to compose, because it contains sensitive information that will be disagreeable to many veterans. Please know my intent was not to show any Veterans Service Organization (VSO) in a negative light. At the same time, my obligation is to the veteran, so I have pulled no punches in accurately presenting this material.

Damn the torpedoes!

The majority of veterans will dismiss me outright when they read this chapter, simply because we vets have been cleverly reared and taught by a very slick marketing and PR machine that VSOs are here to help veterans and act as our liaisons with the VA.

This notion is partly true, in that some VSOs were originally created to aid vets. Somewhere along the way, though, these VSOs were hijacked by the powers that be and turned into organizations that do as little as possible to help the vet in his case against the VA, while creating a friendly atmosphere to project their "usefulness" to veterans.

Some of these organizations even have their own bars and restaurants where vets gather to talk shop and share war stories, or lament over their VA disability claims and appeals cases. These vets are often very loyal to VSOs, and will defend them when attacked by outsiders or when their integrity is questioned by researchers and authors like me.

If you disagree with these statements, just look at the results over the years:

- All VSOs have poorly trained representatives who are *not* experts in VA law, disability claims/appeals case law; VA manuals, guides and regulations; Title 38 of the US Code; Code of Federal Regulations; decisions of the US Court of Appeals for Veterans Claims, US Court of Appeals for the Federal Circuit, and the Supreme Court; the VA's official website and its contents as it pertains to my claim or appeal; the VA's *Federal Benefits for Veterans, Dependents, and Survivors*; West's Veterans Appeals Reporter; and the *Veterans Benefits Manual.*
- VSO representatives are required to undergo only a few hours of training on VA guidelines, but these reps are not skilled in preparing an entire disability claim, even simple ones.
- VSO representatives can handle only simple disability claims cases, and do not fare any better than veterans representing themselves at the Board of Veterans Appeals or US Court of Appeals for Veterans Claims, although both the VA and VSOs

advertise that VSOs fare much better than a veteran acting on his own behalf.

- VSO representatives do not understand and appreciate complex legal and medical issues that many veterans experience.
- Each average VSO representative handles thousands of veterans' disability cases and cannot possibly put in sufficient time and effort to assemble a good case for every veteran, let alone even a few each month.
- The best a VSO representative can do on behalf of a veteran is to assist in downloading and filling out VA forms, and then assisting in submitting completed forms to a VA regional office.
- It is possible that the VSO is not responsible for any errors or omissions when they file a claim or appeal on your behalf. If you challenged the VSO, you would have to file a malpractice claim, which entails hiring a malpractice attorney who may charge you a lot of money unless representing you on a *pro bono* or contingency basis.
- When the VA passed a law in 2007, allowing qualified attorneys to represent veterans after the filing of a Notice of Disagreement, VSOs across the country vehemently opposed the move, because it meant VSOs would lose out on the ability to represent a veteran, sign him/her up as a paying member, and gain further national recognition for "assisting another veteran."
- Chartered VSOs and other VA-recognized organizations are allowed by law to assist veterans

in preparing and filing a VA disability claim from the very beginning of the process, but an attorney is not allowed to represent a veteran at this stage of the process. An attorney can only be hired after a Notice of Disagreement has been filed. The exception, of course, is to hire an attorney to assist you in getting all the right paperwork and forms, then helping you fill them out accurately so you can present them to the VA. What does all this tell you? It suggests all too loudly that the VA knows the ineffectiveness of VSO representation, which will not represent a veteran any better than a vet representing himself, and which will ultimately lead to an immediate denial of a claim. Note that most claims are not appealed, which is what the VA banks on.

- If VSOs were winning the majority of cases against the VA, would the VA continue to support them as it currently does? Would the VA allow VSOs to have cushy offices and suites on VA grounds and in VA Regional Offices? Look at it another way: would you pay the fees and cost of your adversary's attorney, so he could beat you in court? That's not just beyond reason. It is plain stupid.

Many veterans join a VSO and pay dues each year. Each VSO spends considerable funds on advertising and promoting its patriotic image, but fails to inform veterans about how little knowledge they actually possess, how ineffective they actually are in assisting veterans with claims and appeals, how many thousands of veterans each VSO representative or case officer handles at any one time, and how poorly the VSO fares in handling cases at the Board of Veterans Appeals and US Court of Appeals for Veterans Claims.

Yet these VSOs march onward with all the pomp and circumstance of a president inauguration, and continue to represent veterans under false and misleading pretenses that often lead to failed claims and appeals. In the end, these VSOs do more harm than good to veterans, and should be relegated to assisting only with downloading and filling out simple VA forms and then submitting them to VA regional offices.

If you continue to dismiss these facts and wish to sign over power of attorney to a VSO, then please ask the prospective VSO representative the following important questions:

- Are you an expert in VA disability case law?
- How many years have you practiced VA disability law?
- Do you know the top 25 VA cases that are most important to veterans' claims?
- Can you appeal to the board of correction for my service branch to upgrade my less than honorable discharge, so I can apply for disability benefits?
- Have you successfully represented veterans at the Board of Veterans Appeals and US Court of Appeals for Veterans Claims?
- If so, how many successful claims?
- How many losses?
- Have you represented veterans with Decision

Review Officers at your local VA Regional Office?

- If so, how many were successful claims that did not go to appeal?
- How many losses?
- How familiar are you with VA law, disability claims/appeals case law; VA manuals, guides and regulations; Title 38 of the US Code; Code of Federal Regulations; decisions of the US Court of Appeals for Veterans Claims, US Court of Appeals for the Federal Circuit, and the Supreme Court; the VA's official website and its contents as it pertains to my claim or appeal; the VA's *Federal Benefits for Veterans, Dependents, and Survivors*; West's Veterans Appeals Reporter; and the *Veterans Benefits Manual*?
- Do you understand all the legal and medical issues of my case?
- Can you help me get my military records, medical records, and any notes from physicians or specialists to help my claim or appeal?
- If not, how will you represent me and assist in presenting the best possible evidence for my case or appeal?
- Would you talk directly with the Decision Review Officer (DRO) for my case?
- How much time will you put into assisting me develop my claim or appeal?
- If I choose to have a hearing at the Board of Veterans Appeals in Washington, DC, will you travel with me?

- If so, what will it cost me to have you there as my representative?
- If not, will you be present at my VA Regional Office hearing?
- If errors are made by you in my case that result in my being denied VA benefits, how will you rectify your errors?
- Will you take full legal responsibility for the loss of my case?
- Will it cost me additional money if you cause errors in my case?
- Who will be held responsible if there are errors or omissions in my file?
- Are you an excellent, effective and persuasive writer, so that you will write any letters or information on claims/appeals form on my behalf?
- How many hours of training do you have on VA disability claims and appeals, VA case law, policies and procedures?
- How many additional hours of training do you get each year on the preceding subjects?
- Do you attend training seminars offered by the National Organization of Veterans' Advocates?
- If a typical DRO has thousands of pages of paperwork, books, manuals, etc. to study and consider for a typical case, and clearly never has the time to do so, how can you possibly do the same on my behalf, especially since you represent thousands of other veterans?
- How often each week will you be available to

work with me on my claim or appeal until it is successfully completed and submitted to my VA Regional Office?
- Will you take the time to help me fully understand my claim or appeal?
- Can you get me an earlier effective date for my disability claim?

If you decide to have a VSO represent you in your claim or appeal, you must have the VSO file VA Form 21-22, Appointment of Veterans Service Organization as Claimant's Representative, directly with your VA Regional Office. This gives your new VSO the power to represent you in preparing, presenting and prosecuting claims and appeals under VA law.

Choose carefully if you go this route. Do not choose a VSO simply because your buddy told you to. Each VA disability claim and appeal is different and, just because one servicemember or veteran received a favorable decision, does not mean you will, too.

You must protect yourself from incompetent or incomplete representation. If your goal is simply to have someone help you locate and fill out VA forms, then a VSO will normally do that with little difficulty.

There are thousands of anecdotal instances where a VSO mismanaged a veteran's disability claim or appeal and thus committed egregious malpractice. In almost all of those instances, the veteran was left with a denied claim or appeal and was not allowed by law to pursue his case further.

If you have a complex disability case or appeal, and you

do not understand the case or your rights, then you need an expert who will take the time to read your entire file, and prepare and present an accurate disability claim or appeal on your behalf.

Simply put, no VSO can perform this on your behalf. The system is too complex, VSO representatives are too overworked, and you will never get the assistance required to present and win your claim or appeal.

The only possibility is to hire someone who is an expert in the entire VA disability claims and appeals process, who has many years of proven experience, who has won a significant number of these cases, and who fully understands your case, and who can explain it to you so you feel comfortable with the process. In almost all cases, this is an attorney who is an expert in all aspects of preparing, presenting and prosecuting a disability claim or appeal.

In the end, you must ask yourself some tough questions:

- Am I capable of handling my disability claim or appeal on my own?
- If not, do I fully trust a VSO to represent me successfully on my claim or appeal?
- Have I done exhaustive research on whether to have either a VSO representative or hire an attorney to represent me?

You have already served your fellow men and women, received an honorable discharge from the US military and the toughest and most demanding and dangerous job you have ever had or will have. Now it's time to have an expert take care of your disability claim or appeal. Please think very carefully on how you will approach this sensitive subject, because your choice will affect you for years to come.

If you follow the excellent advice of men and women who have gone before you, those who advocated having an experienced attorney represent you, then you have a good chance of succeeding where the majority of men and women fail.

Final Notes on *Veterans Service Organizations*:

1. Understand the facts about VSOs, how they are designed, how they operate, where their funds come from, how much of their funds actually goes to assisting veterans, the type and complexity of relevant training VSO representatives receive each year, and how little VSOs actually assist veterans in complex disability claim and appeal cases.

2. Dismiss your own sense of patriotism when considering using a VSO to represent you in the claims or appeals process. VSOs are designed and built by expensive and slick marketing and PR machines that have created an impressive organization that looks and feels like an advocate for veterans, but in reality is merely an advocate for the VA.

3. When it comes to your claim or appeal, you must consider using only the best possible advocate, which is a highly experienced attorney or law firm. Even the most popular VSO is no substitute, regardless of all the strong, positive advertising presented by that VSO.

4. The most important items in VA disability claims and appeals are: VA law, disability claims/appeals case law; VA manuals, guides and regulations; Title 38 of the US Code; Code of Federal Regulations; decisions of the US Court

of Appeals for Veterans Claims, US Court of Appeals for the Federal Circuit, and the Supreme Court; the VA's official website and its contents as it pertains to my claim or appeal; the VA's *Federal Benefits for Veterans, Dependents, and Survivors*; West's Veterans Appeals Reporter; and the *Veterans Benefits Manual.* If your prospective representative is not an expert in the all the above, then keep looking until you find one.

Q&A

Practically every patriotic American says VSOs are the best type of representation in VA disability claims and appeals cases. Is it true?

If by "best" you mean they have great advertising, marketing and PR that makes them *appear* effective, like they help veterans with their disability claims and appeals, then, yes.

But when you examine their efficacy in representing veterans in the VA disability claims and appeals process, they fare no better than any other VSO: poorly. The results speak louder than any slick advertising, marketing and PR campaign ever could: these VSOs are great at making themselves look good, paying their CEOs and executive officers too much money at the expense of veterans, falsely advertising their effectiveness as veterans' advocates, and providing false and misleading and harmful representation to veterans.

If I'm filing a VA disability claim for the first time, where do I go for help?

Some VSOs are good at assisting a veteran with filing an initial claim, provided the vet has already assembled his/her claims package to include service records, medical records, list of injuries with dates and proof (medical records), relevant statements from physicians and buddies, etc. It is up to the vet to have a complete package before going to a VSO, which will help the vet download, fill out and file the correct form(s) to submit to the vet's VA Regional Office.

If a vet is filing for the first time and is completely ignorant of the whole VA disability claims process, then it is wise to get legal advice from an attorney who can assist the vet in gathering all necessary information and then submitting it to the regional office. It is okay for the vet to hire an attorney to assist in *preparing* a claim, but the vet must be the one to actually file the claim with his/her VA Regional Office.

The VA cannot dictate who assists the vet when assembling and preparing a VA disability claim, but it does not allow a vet to have an attorney represent him/her against the VA until after a Notice of Disagreement has been filed with the VA.

Again, anyone can assist the vet prepare a disability case file, but the vet should have someone who is an expert in the initial VA disability claims process and who knows exactly what materials are required, how they are assembled, and where and when to file the completed package.

6

INTRODUCTION TO THE APPEAL PROCESS

If you are reading this chapter, it is because the VA denied your claim and you would like some guidance about how to appeal the VA's decision.

In this chapter, I explain in relative detail all the steps of the appeal process, but this chapter's information is by no means exhaustive. I recommend having on hand Mr. John Roche's two books on VA claims and appeals, *The Veteran's Survival Guide: How to File and Collect on VA Claims*, Second Edition and *Claim Denied!*, both of which are referenced at the end of this book.

Mr. Roche goes into great detail on the history of claims and appeals, some of which may be useful to you. He also details how relevant VA employees do their jobs at different stages of the claims and appeals process, so you can better understand those opposing you and your claim or appeal. A word of caution here: Mr. Roche's books were last printed in

2006 and, since he passed away in 2012, some information is sadly out of date. If you read my work and then find something contrary or different in Mr. Roche's books, I suggest you make every attempt to corroborate what I have stated in this current book. My research findings and statements are up to date, as of Veterans Day 2015, about a year after the date when the VA made a major announcement about how veterans will be filing disability claims. The VA stated they will now use a standard form, VA Form 21-526EZ.

I also highly recommend buying *Navigating Legal Issues for Military Veterans: Leading Lawyers On Arguing Disability, Pension, and Other Claims Before the VA*, authored by seven different experts on the VA disability claims and appeals process. Like Mr. Roche's books, this has valuable information and details about the claims and appeals process that you will not find anywhere else. But, like all books on this subject, the material is not exhaustive.

You will not find everything you need to know all in one book or manual. The VA claims and appeals process is just too complex.

However, these three books, along with my *VA Disability Claim*, will give you the best possible introduction to this whole claims and appeals process. Plus, I update my book as soon as the VA makes changes to the claims and appeals process. For example, on 24 September 2014, I received the VA's press release about VA Form 21-526EZ, and immediately updated this book and uploaded the new file to Amazon.com and the ebook to my website. I'm certain this will not be the last change this year but, rest assured, when they come, I will be there to roll with the changes and share them with you.

Before I introduce the specific steps and details of the actual appeal process, I offer some helpful advice you should strongly consider, because it has assisted many a veteran in getting satisfactory disability benefits. Plus, and I cannot stress this point enough, please get yourself an excellent, VA-accredited attorney to handle your appeal. As I outline below, having a VSO handle your appeal is a disaster waiting to happen, especially if your case is medically and legally complex.

By far, the most difficult part of the entire VA disability claims and appeals process is the *appeal*. Unfortunately, almost all veterans are thrust into this area, their claims having been denied, but few actually continue the fight and file an appeal. They simply quit, rather than endure the passive-aggressive wrath, disrespect, lying, cheating, malfeasance and malpractice of the VA.

Honestly, how much different is the VA monster than the enemies you fought against while in service? After years of hardship as a servicemember, were you expecting the VA to take good care of you, as advertised and marketed by the VA's hired guns? If so, your expectations were inaccurate and certainly not met.

Get A VA-Accredited Law Firm To Represent You

It is absolutely essential to have good, sound legal representation during the entire appeal process, because an experienced, VA-accredited attorney will know all the laws, rules and regulations that the VA is using to deny your claim, and, most important, your attorney will know how to fight the VA and beat it at its own game. The VA is fighting against you every step of the way, so you need good legal representation to fight back.

Do not use an attorney who is not accredited by the VA. If you go to your neighborhood attorney because she offers free "advice," but she is not accredited by the VA and is not an expert in VA disability claims and appeals, then you will get poor advice. Would you go to a podiatrist (foot doctor) if you needed complex brain surgery? What's worse, if you act on that poor advice, you may harm or even lose your appeal.

Again, hire a VA-accredited attorney.

Anyone who goes up against the VA without legal representation has convinced himself that he has the legal and medical prowess to defeat a giant machine that has an army of judges, lawyers, paralegals, law clerks, doctors, nurses, technicians, etc., all of whom are prepared to work against you. They do this all the time and they're good at it. And still you think you can go head to head with this beast?

Before you talk with an attorney, know that this is a highly specialized field of study and practice, and there are very few good VA-accredited attorneys with an excellent track record. When you do your due diligence on these prospective attorneys, ask some hard questions. These are only suggestions that will yield important information about your prospective attorney. You may have some of your own, so do not be afraid to ask anything you feel is relevant.

- Are you a VA-accredited attorney? Since what date?

- Are you actively practicing VA disability claims and appeals law? How long?
- When was the last case you handled? Was it successful, i.e. did you win?
- How many cases have you handled? Of those VA cases, how many have you won?
- What fees do you charge a veteran? Are you willing to take my case for 20% and not 33.3%? If not, why?
- How often do you undergo veterans law training, and what credentials (e.g. Continuing Education credits) do you have?
- How many VA disability claims or appeals cases are you currently handling?
- Are you willing to put in the necessary time to ensure I receive the highest possible disability rating and retro award?
- Can you assist me in getting an earlier effective date for my benefits?
- How far are you willing to represent me in my appeal? Will you go to the US Court of Appeals for Veterans Claims and, if necessary, the Court of Appeals for the Federal Circuit, and the US Supreme Court?
- Are you admitted to practice before the US Court of Appeals for Veterans Claims, the Court of Appeals for the Federal Circuit, and the US Supreme Court?

It is best to have your case prepared in advance, so your prospective attorney can see the whole picture quickly and evaluate it. If he thinks he would have to wade through hundred of documents just to determine your case, he will tell you thanks, but no thanks. Or, if he sees that he might have a good case, he might suggest that you go back and organize your files and assemble a good case for him to review.

When you talk with a law firm or attorney for the first time, they'll put you through their intake process with a clerk who is not an attorney but can evaluate your case in very simple terms.

All law firms and attorneys have minimum criteria that must be met before they take a case. Please note that case evaluations may differ among attorneys and law firms:

- When did the veteran file the Notice of Disagreement?
- Does the case have merit: are there specific or even broad issues in the veteran's case that can be successfully argued and thus make the case winnable?
- Does the veteran have a case that has sufficient precedents to back up the case?
- Will winning the case produce sufficient money for the firm or attorney?

There are many other criteria attorneys and law firms may use to evaluate your case, and you have no say about those criteria. The plain fact is, if you have a good case that is well documented, you have a good chance of securing an attorney or law firm to represent you in your appeal.

Your first visit to, or phone call with, an attorney should be your best sales pitch: have an accurate, brief and concise document or, if via the phone, description that describes your condition, when it happened in service, medical treatments in service and following discharge, what type of disabilities you originally filed for, and any correspondence from the VA that shows how the VA responded to your claim for benefits. If you talked with an attorney or clerk on the phone, they will have you fax or send the above documents to their office for review. Many attorneys and law firms will also want to see your C-file, which is the VA's complete file on your disability claim or appeal. If you already have your C-file, make multiple copies of it and then update those copies as necessary.

If an attorney or law firm agrees to represent you, they will send you an agreement that also states the various fees they are entitled to receive from you. The VA limits a law firm's or attorney's fees to 33.3% of an award. If your case is excellent, and the firm or attorney has a history of winning tough cases, then agree to their terms, because getting 66.7% of the award is better than 0%.

Your new attorney also will have you sign VA Form 21–22a, which notifies the VA that you are allowing them to represent you.

It is unlikely that you will win your appeal without good legal representation, unless you become an expert at VA case law and can use the VA's various arcane laws, rules and reg's against them. This is a steep learning curve and requires years of hard work, experience and patience and money, but it can be done. Some enterprising veterans have taken their own cases to appellate courts and won, but this is a rare occurrence.

In my case, I represented myself for 15 years and was able

to get a 60% service-connected disability rating. But when I tried to get an increase, plus include secondary injuries that arose from my primary service-connected injuries, I ran into a stone wall. That's when I hired an excellent attorney to take over and see my case through to the end. Without this law firm, I would have failed again and again, gone into a deeper depression, and . . . who knows how I would have ended up?

A VSO Is Not Likely To Help You Win Your Case

Some veterans swear by their VSO, because their representative was able to perform relatively simple duties to get the veteran an acceptable disability rating. Most veterans, however, are not satisfied with their VSOs, but were not able to secure a competent attorney to represent them, so they stuck with the VSO throughout the appeals process. And in the end felt they were poorly represented and ripped off, not only by the VA but by their VSO.

According to the latest published statistics by the Board of Veterans' Appeals, approximately 85% of veterans' appeals are represented by VSOs. The remainder are represented either by an attorney or other individual, or no one at all.

Interestingly, the VA openly suggests all veterans use a VSO during the initial claims process. But they make no suggestions whatsoever for the appeals process.

Curious, isn't it? But what does it tell us?

Simply put, the VA secretly has a cozy relationship with all federally chartered VSOs, most of whom have offices on VA property, and also secretly knows that those VSOs will only do so much on behalf of veterans. Many of these VSOs are funded directly by the government, allowing them to hire officers and representatives to assist veterans, although the training these VSO representatives receive is inadequate at best.

Furthermore, the VA knows these VSOs will not be the formidable challengers like attorneys and law firms, which are not allowed to have offices on VA property and are not afforded the cozy perks that VSOs receive from the VA.

Even if you do not subscribe to these facts, please examine the results yourself: go to your VA Regional Office and look around. Are there any legal firms in the Office? How many VSOs are there? Do these VSOs have access to the VA's Stakeholder Enterprise Portal (SEP), a computer-based system that permits VSOs to submit documentation for veterans' disability cases. Can these VSOs upload new information about a veteran's claim or appeal? Does it look like these VSOs and their officers and representatives blend in nicely with their VA surroundings?

C'mon, be honest with yourself here. . . .

As of August 2014, attorneys and law firms are not allowed access to SEP; only VSOs are permitted access to the system and to training on SEP by the VA. Attorneys must submit almost all documentation on behalf of veterans' claims via various forms of mail (FedEx, UPS, US Postal Service, courier, hand-deliver, etc.).

The VA has stated that, sometime in the future, "education providers, doctors, attorneys, loan appraisers, benefit providers, and others" will have access to SEP.

In general, the most a VSO will do is ask for another C&P exam or lightly contest the outcome of a previous exam. Remember, the VA allows federally chartered VSOs to have offices in VA Regional Offices and in other areas on VA property. No VSO would dare overstep the bounds of this mutually beneficial agreement.

A poignant example: a VSO was representing a veteran in the appeals process, and promised the veteran he would ask for another C&P exam because the VSO agreed that the previous one was flawed and not even completed. When the deadline neared, the VSO representative chose not go to the Decision Review Officer, because, as he told the veteran, "Look, I didn't want to piss her off. We have a good working relationship, you know?"

The result? The DRO denied the veteran's appeal, closed the file, and sent it back to the Board of Veterans Appeals.

Get an experienced law firm or attorney to handle your case. Do not leave it to amateur VSO representatives to assist you in your VA disability appeal, no matter how well-meaning, patriotic, kind and respectful VSO representatives appear to be, what they promise you, or how well they treat you and your family.

Final Notes on *Introduction To The Appeal Process*:

1. It is absolutely essential that you buy the three books I suggested at the beginning of this chapter, because they are the only ones in existence that provide the best possible resources on filing claims and appeals with the VA. In my book, ***VA Disability Claim***, I provide details taken from hundreds of different resources. If you had to do the research on your own, it would take hundreds of hours, plus additional time digesting the information and making sense of it. I have distilled it down to the bare essence and have put it in

language that is easy to understand, plus included easy-to-follow steps.

2. The greatest gift you can give yourself is to get yourself a VA-accredited attorney. It took me more than a dozen years before I secured the services of one. If I'd hired my attorney early on in the process, I would have saved myself many years of heartache. And that is no exaggeration. I have provided some starting questions to ask prospective attorneys, so please take full advantage of them in finding one who is right for you.

3. I have already stated this previously, but it bears repeating: a VSO is not likely to help you win your case, because they are not nearly as trained and skilled as an attorney. I've yet to see an exception, after meeting and talking with more than 2,500 servicemembers and veterans over the years about the VA claims and appeals process. You may talk with a vet whose claim was simple, say, an injury to his lower leg because of a bad parachute landing, and discover that he got a 40% disability rating from the VA with the assistance of his VSO representative.

This sounds impressive, until you learn that the vet's injuries have lead to other complications that have rendered him unable to walk on that leg. And now he has to file for additional injuries that have not even been certified service-connected. If he had used an experienced attorney, that vet would have filed an appeal for additional disabilities and earned a higher rating. Now he has to begin the process all over again, with a new effective date, all because the VSO representative failed to note additional injuries and did not file an appeal after the initial 40% rating was handed down.

Q&A

Why are telling me to spend my hard-earned money on all these books? Can't I just find the information on my own?

If you choose to re-invent the wheel, have at it. I did it many times over during my VA claims and appeals. As I look back on it, it was a nightmare. But I have no regrets because I became an expert in the process and am now able to share my knowledge with others. If you want to go the route I did, I commend you. But if you wish to get the highest disability rating possible without having to find all the information yourself and spend years of heartache doing it, then I recommend your buying the books I suggested, getting a VA-accredited attorney at the earliest possible moment to assist in filing your claim, and learning what is necessary to maintain your claim and appeal.

Can I use my wife's sister, who is a real estate attorney?

No. VA law is a specific and complex field and you must have an attorney who is knowledgeable and experienced in all aspects of the VA claims and appeals process. No other type of attorney can assist you adequately in this process. When you are first filing your claim, a non-VA-accredited attorney can assist you in finding out where to get the necessary forms, but so can a VSO representative. A VA-accredited attorney know all steps of the process, so please use him.

Besides, the law states you can use only a VA-accredited attorney.

7

STEPS AND DETAILS OF THE APPEAL PROCESS

If your claim for disability benefits is denied by your regional office, they will send a detailed notice, stating they have denied your claim, why they denied it, and what your options are.

If you wish to pursue an appeal, you must file the new VA Form 21-0958 (Notice of Disagreement, NOD) within one year from the date the rating decision was mailed to you.

You also have the option of simply writing your NOD on toilet paper, which would certainly send a strong message to the VA. They also must accept this colorful form of NOD, but I highly recommend using VA Form 21-0958, which may expedite your claim or, in the very least, not hinder its progress.

That beginning date is usually hand-stamped on your

denial letter, and appears somewhere at the top of the cover letter the VA sent you. If there is no date present, notify the VA or your representative immediately, so you receive the most accurate date.

If you miss this one-year deadline, then the decision of the Decision Review Officer becomes final and you lose your ability to appeal your claim.

You do have the option of writing to your regional office and requesting an extension of the one-year deadlines. In the letter, you must explain that you need additional time to discover, develop and present your evidence, and that you absolutely need more than one year. You should ask for an additional six months, if not longer.

You can also use VA Form 21-4138, the Statement in Support of Claim, but I still recommend following the VA's new guideline of filing VA Form 21-0958 (NOD).

The new NOD, VA Form 21-0958, now allows you to list specific details of what you disagree with and why, plus what percentage disability you are seeking.

When filing your VA Form 21-0958, please do so at the earliest possible date.

I suggest you think carefully before sending any letter out, especially if you are disappointed or angry, because your level of objectivity and clarity will be poor. Please give yourself some time to cool down, then consult an attorney about how best to file the NOD.

Remember, there is a human being on the other end of your NOD, and if you write something offensive and lacking in objectivity, the person reading your statement may just file it at the bottom of the pile or, worse, "misplace" it.

You also should follow up once a month, if not more, to ensure the VA has received your NOD and is indeed working your case.

This ends the first stage of the appeal process, so sit back and wait patiently for the VA to issue you its response to your NOD.

Once the VA has received your NOD, it will issue an "appeal process request letter," which gives you two options for appealing the VA's decision: 1. You can opt to have a Decision Review Officer (DRO) review your case; or 2. Go through the traditional appeal process, which entails going to the Board of Veterans' Appeals.

If you choose the DRO route, the VA will send you a "decision review process letter." After some time, the DRO will make a decision on your case and send you a Statement of the Case (SOC), which explains the DRO's decision in full, thus allowing you and your attorney to file a substantive appeal. You or your attorney can file your appeal to the regional office within 60 days of the date of the SOC or opt to file within one year from the original date the VA sent you its letter denying your claim.

The DRO also will send a VA Form 9, which is an Appeal to the Board of Veterans' Appeals (BVA). If you are unsatisfied with the DRO's decision, then you will file VA Form 9.

The substantive appeal should consist of VA Form 9, plus a

document that states that the appeal is being "perfected" and all issues are being considered, VA errors of fact and law are argued, and any other supporting information is included.

You must file VA Form 9, the Substantive Appeal, with your regional office within one year from the date stamped on your decision of denied benefits. The DRO will review your case and "certify" that it is ready for consideration by the BVA.

It is possible that the VA may dismiss your appeal outright for failing to properly file the substantive appeal, but this is unlikely if you have an attorney to represent and guide you. Nonetheless, if the VA dismisses your appeal because of this, you or your attorney can appeal this decision.

At this stage, you definitely should have legal representation who can assist you in preparing an excellent supporting document to file with Form 9.

Some important items to consider:

1. You must thoroughly review the VA's SOC to ensure the VA considered all the evidence and supporting information you submitted.
2. Go over the findings of your C&P exam(s) the VA used in helping it determine the extent of your injuries. Do you agree with the findings? If not, do you have evidence to show otherwise? You must gather this evidence so you can state why you disagree with the results of the C&P exam.
3. It is most important to review the final few pages of the SOC, which justifies why the VA denied

your claim. The statements made by the VA can be important and pivotal starting points for your appeal, so pay close attention.

4. An experienced VA-accredited attorney is an excellent resource during this stage, so use him wisely. He will read and discover things that you will surely miss or fail to understand or appreciate the importance of.

5. An attorney also can assist in assembling all the evidence you will need to file the complete supporting documentation to accompany VA Form 9. You should carefully study the entire file the VA has on your case, including all sworn statements, letters from outside physicians and experts, medical facts and associated laws that support them, C&P exam results, and your entire service record and medical records.

6. Your attorney will examine all the evidence and determine whether you will need additional supporting evidence like medical exams from outside doctors or experts.

7. Once you and your attorney have collected all the evidence, he will assemble an excellent argument in your favor, citing relevant case law or pointing out all the errors the VA made in its deciding your claim, including its faulty conclusions.

Once the BVA receives your VA Form 9 and associated documentation, it issues a "docket notification letter" and states that your appeal has been added to the docket. Please note that your appeal is now in "docket order," which means your case will be reviewed in the order in which it was docketed.

It now takes about 18-24 months for your appeal to be heard by the BVA. You and/or your attorney have the option of traveling to Washington, DC, to present your case. Most good attorneys will choose this option, because they can freely argue all the point of your case in front of a BVA judge, and even add additional, last-minute information that may not be possible otherwise.

It can take several years for the BVA to render a final decision on your appeal, so be prepared to exercise the greatest level of patience during this period. It's best to put the entire appeal out of your mind at this point, and find something meaningful to do. You should periodically call to check the status of your claim: (202) 565-5436.

BVA decisions are final, except in cases of remand, where the BVA returns your case to the regional office for further study, to gather additional evidence, or to reconsider certain issues. In remanded claims, the DRO for your appeal must provide special care and handling and complete the review as soon as possible. Some refer to this as "fast-tracking" a file. Once the DRO has completed your file, he re-certifies it and send it back to the BVA to render a decision.

In the end, the BVA will either grant, deny or remand your claim. If you have any questions at all after the BVA returns its decision, you can email the Appeals Management Center: amcdirmailbox@va.gov.

If you are not happy with the BVA's decision, you and/or attorney can appeal to the US Court of Appeals for Veterans

Claims (CAVC). According to the CAVC, "The Court has exclusive jurisdiction over decisions of the Board of Veterans' Appeals. The Court reviews BVA decisions appealed by claimants who believe the BVA erred in its decision. The Court's review of BVA decisions is based on the record before the agency and arguments of the parties, which are presented in a written brief, with oral argument generally held only in cases presenting new legal issues."

After receiving the BVA's final decision, you or your attorney can file a Notice of Appeal (NOA) with the CAVC within 120 days after the mailing date of the BVA's unfavorable decision. Many veterans choose to go this route, but they are at a severe disadvantage without the counsel of an experienced attorney.

According to the CAVC, you must mail your NOA to "Clerk, US Court of Appeals for Veterans Claims, 625 Indiana Avenue, NW, Suite 900, Washington, DC 20004-2950.

"The NOA will be timely if it is properly addressed to the Court and bears a legible postmark affixed by the United States Postal Service (USPS) within 120 days after the mailing date of the BVA decision that you are appealing. A postage-metered date imprint other than one affixed by USPS does not qualify.

"You may send this NOA by facsimile transmission to (202) 501-5848 or by means other than US mail. If you do that, or if you mail the NOA and it does not bear a legible USPS postmark, the NOA will be late if it arrives at the

Court after the 120-day time limit.

"There is a $50 filing fee for an appeal. Send a check or money order, payable to 'US Court of Appeals for Veterans Claims,' with this NOA. Do not send cash. To request a waiver of the filing fee, attach a completed Form 4 (Declaration of Financial Hardship)."

The CAVC is not a trial court; its actions exist largely on paper. The CAVC does not allow witness testimony or the introduction of new evidence. Know that the VA has an army of legal representation, including trained attorneys who will fight you tooth and nail and ask the CAVC to uphold the BVA's original decision on your appeal. Historically, the CAVC issues decisions decided by a single judge who will either agree with the BVA's decision, reverse that decision, or vacate (legally void) the BVA's decision and remand your appeal to the BVA for further work and adjudication. According to the latest statistics, CAVC rarely reverses the BVA's decisions, but they can always issue a remand, which means your appeal goes back to the BVA.

As with all other stages of the appeal process, you must pay special attention to any deadlines for submitting forms and information to the CAVC.

If the CAVC upholds the BVA's decision to deny your appeal, then you or your attorney may file an appeal with the US Court of Appeals for the Federal Circuit (CAFC), which has exclusive jurisdiction over decisions made by the CAVC.

The CAFC will not review any findings of fact. It can

only review the legal means by which the Veterans Court interpreted applicable statutes and regulations in your appeal. It is not entirely clear why, but most cases appealed to the CAFC are dismissed. Check with an attorney first before pursuing this option, given that almost all appeals are dismissed by the CAFC, which suggests there are some very specific rules and procedures one must follow to get a favorable decision by the CAFC.

It is thought that most dismissals result from careless mistakes made by an appellant (you, defending yourself *pro se*) or attorney. According to the CAFC, the following are the top 10 reasons why briefs are rejected:

1. Proof of Service: A proof of service does not accompany the Appendix. (Fed. R. App. P. 25(d))
2. Font Size of Footnotes: footnotes are not printed in the same size font as the text of the brief. (Fed. R. App. P. 32(a)(5) and Practice Note to Rule 32)
3. Certificate of Interest: the brief does not contain a certificate of interest. (Fed. Cir. R. 28(a)(1))
4. Official Caption: the cover of the brief does not follow the official caption provided by the Clerk. (Fed. R. App. P. 32(a)(2)(A-D) A copy of the official caption is included with the notice of docketing)
5. Impermissible Addendum: the brief contains an impermissible addendum. Excluding the required addendum in the Appellant or Petitioner's brief, an addendum attached to any other brief is acceptable if it contains only statutes, rules, regulations, etc. (Fed. R. App. P. 28(f))
6. Confidential Material Deleted: the Table of

Contents of any nonconfidential brief or appendix must describe the general nature of the confidential material that has been deleted. (Fed. Cir. R. 28(d)(1)(B) and 30(h)(1)(B); an example is in Practice Note 28)
7. Judgment, Order, or Decision in Question: the Appellant or Petitioner's brief does not contain the judgment, order, or decision in question as an addendum placed within the brief. (Fed. Cir. R. 28(a)(12))
8. Statement of Related Cases: the brief does not contain a statement of related cases. (Fed. Cir. R. 28(a)(4) and 47.5)
9. Table of Contents in Appendix: the appendix must begin with a table of contents identifying the page at which each part begins. (Fed. R. App. P. 30(d))
10. Combined Brief and Appendix: when the brief and appendix are combined, the cover must so indicate. Fed. Cir. R. 30(d)(1))

Finally, for the intrepid souls whose appeal was dismissed by the CAFC, there is the US Supreme Court.

Only attorneys who are certified to practice in front of the Supreme Court may present a case, and those are all experienced, so you should have excellent legal representation before you apply, let alone present your case. It goes without saying that the decision of this Court on your appeal is final.

Final Notes on *The Appeal Process*:

1. The VA calls the appeal process "adversarial," which suggests that the preceding claims process is friendly. The VA's powerful and persuasive publicity machine has fooled most Americans into thinking the VA is a benevolent organization that assists and cares for US veterans, especially during the claims process.

A law was even passed that mandated that the VA would assist veterans: The Duty To Assist Law (38 U.S. Code § 5103A - *Duty to assist claimants*). Unfortunately, the VA does next to nothing in its "duty to assist" veterans, because, as various VA executives have claimed in Congressional hearings, there aren't enough man-hours to assist all veterans in the claims and appeals process.

And when the VA has "assisted" veterans in the claims and appeals process, the VA has often omitted documents from veterans' service and medical records, provided false or fraudulent information that was detrimental to veterans' cases, etc.

Mark my word: the entire VA disability claims and appeals process is *100% adversarial*, so you must have an excellent case to present to the VA. If you choose to go it alone, good luck.

I highly recommend your hiring an excellent attorney who is well familiar with VA disability claims and appeals cases and who has an excellent track record at the VA Regional Office level, and with the Board of Veterans Appeals, US Court of Appeals for Veterans Claims, the Court of Appeals for the Federal Circuit, and the US Supreme Court.

The most thoughtful, well-planned and presented appeals

to a regional office are the ones that received the most favorable decisions. In short, if you do your homework, pay close attention to all the details of your case and relevant case law, and have an excellent attorney to at least advise you on legal matters, then you can prevail in your appeal without spending an additional 10 years slaving away in the extended appeal process like many of us have done.

Q&A

How do I find someone to help me gather all the facts and evidence for my appeal?

Many veterans have done it all on their own, because they were experienced at doing research and gathering evidence. As stated several times in this chapter, I strongly recommend that you start looking for an attorney the moment you receive a letter of denial from the VA, if not sooner. Almost all claims are denied outright by the VA, so I would start researching VA-accredited law firms and attorneys sooner.

If you choose to go about your appeal on your own, then you are in for a long, hard ride. You must learn how to locate and assemble all your service and medical records, learn VA law and case law for appeals, learn how to write and present all the necessary VA forms and documents required for your appeal, and how to keep your cool during the entire process, which will take at least several years.

Again, get an attorney who already knows the entire process. You will pay him only when he wins your appeal, and it is possible to have the VA pay all attorney's fees once you win your appeal. Most VA-accredited attorney's will charge 20%, especially if you are indigent or on a low fixed income.

If an attorney wants 33.3%, ask him if he will take your case for 20%, simply because the VA states that anything over 20% is "unfair" to the veteran.

Remember, you pay an attorney only when he wins your appeal, so it's a favorable situation for you during the appeal process, not having to pay any hourly fees to an attorney and thus draining you of all your funds.

Why does the appeal process take so long?

The first chapter of this book states clearly some of the reasons, one of which is that the VA is designed to be an adversarial agent of the US government, one that fights veterans nearly every step of the way, and to provide as few benefits as possible.

To appreciate these facts, all you need do is become a part of the VA system and examine the results over a few years. You will see gross incompetence, mismanagement, ineffectiveness, malpractice, malfeasance, severe lack of quality control, and downright stupidity and poor behavior by VA employees at all levels and in all VA medical centers, hospitals, clinics and offices.

An example, one you probably have experienced: it can take many months for a document you submitted to the VA to move from a mail holding and sorting facility to the proper office.

Would this be acceptable behavior in a Fortune 500 company? Absolutely not. Everyone at the top would be fired, all middle management summarily booted or retrained, and lower employees forced to move on or get substantial retraining on even the most basic duties and responsibilities.

And that is just a simple example. Think about how long it takes to find someone competent to talk with about your claim or appeal. The situation gets worse as you find yourself deeper in the VA system.

No amount of money in the VA's substantial yearly budget will correct any of these problems, as evidenced over the past 10 years with the introduction of new IT offices and protocols, new computer systems and methods of transmitting claims and appeals forms and documents.

The more things change at the VA, the more they stay the same, because of the VA's deeply flawed character, work ethic, and a fundamental distrust of all veterans who file claims and appeals with the VA.

The best you can do to alleviate long wait times and other issues is to keep accurate, up-to-date service and medical records, VA correspondence, copies of claims and appeals you make, and all supporting information and documentation that support your claim or appeal. You also should understand the VA claims and appeals process from beginning at least to the point where you are at the moment, and secure the expert services of a VA-accredited attorney to assist you in your claim or appeal.

Also know that the appeal process will only get worse as more and more active-duty service personnel become veterans and enter the VA system.

HOW TO STAY SANE THROUGHOUT THE ENTIRE PROCESS

Be patient and don't let the bastards get you down. I cannot stress this point enough, because I've seen too many veterans give up in the face of adversity, even though they just got back from fighting on the front lines of Afghanistan or Iraq.

That's the best advice anyone can give you: never quit the VA claims and appeals process.

If you are expecting a quick payout for your service-connected injury, then your expectation does not match what happens in reality. Especially the reality according to the VA.

Have a good support group surrounding you and helping you. If you have a family, this is the time to sit them all down and explain the whole claims and appeal process, and that it may take years to get a favorable rating and retro payment.

Please do not see a retro payment as next month's windfall, because it may not even come at all. And here you are, sitting around waiting for it to fall into your lap.

While you're waiting for a favorable decision, don't get angry at the VA, be proactive and win your case. Ask yourself: did I have all my paperwork in order and was the package 100% clean and legible? Did I file my application correctly? Did I follow up and visit the regional office to ensure the VA had in fact received my completed application, and are they working on it right now? Have I interviewed attorneys who are experts in VA claims and appeals, should something go wrong? Have I looked after myself adequately and set me and my family up for the best possible scenario when the VA comes down with its decision? What did I miss or forget to do or turn in?

Go back and double-check all your work, because the VA is always looking for the smallest excuse to deny your claim or appeal.

The VA is like a sneaky, bratty and malicious child. You must beat the child at its own game, knowing you will never change its behavior, only your own. You must see the VA as it truly is, and conduct yourself professionally at all times, because the VA can and will use anything against you in your claim or appeal, plus it also can strip you of all rights and privileges if you break the law.

The VA is also a company within a larger corporation, The United States of America, Inc. Regardless of whether you believe this, it is 100% accurate and true.

So when you deal with the VA, you must understand how it works and whom it really works for: *not you.* It is a psychopath bent on doing you and your family harm, so you must be armed with the best defense: expert knowledge, patience, time and some extra money for all those mailings.

The VA is set up as a business and operates as such. While it is not necessarily in the business to make a lot of money, it is in the business to prevent veterans from taking the money they are allotted each year by the VA's parent company. Again, if you do not believe this scenario, just look at some of the results of the VA's actions and behaviors over the decades and you will see these distinct and disturbing patterns that all lead to their not being on the side of veterans and their families. If the VA were truly a benevolent organization, committed to helping veterans and their families, then we would see an entirely different VA than we do today. There would be no need for the VA to hire the best advertising, marketing and public-relations firms in the country to improve its image. There would be no need for the VA to lie about its malfeasance and malpractice.

Things would look quite different.

But they don't, so what does this tell you?

Surprisingly, some of VA's executives and middle managers earn huge bonuses, which are contingent upon how many cases they closed in a given period of time for that year. The bosses of those claims reviewers also receive bonuses when their subordinates perform well, so it's in everyone's best interest to "perform well," i.e. deny claims, save the company a lot of money, and close as many claims and appeals cases as possible, make their regional offices look good on paper, and stay out of the national spotlight, especially when things go wrong.

Have something meaningful to do while you await the VA's decision

You should have a regular job that is rewarding and that pays well enough to sustain you and your family through the entire VA claims and appeal process. Working each day is good for the heart, mind, body and soul, so keep busy. Those veterans who are home-bound or confined to a wheelchair are at risk for depression, anxiety and other issues that take their toll over the weeks, months and years.

Without meaningful work or activities, those vets often succumb to the stress and pressures. In these instances, the VA does offer counseling services. If you find them useful, then use them. If not, find an outside therapist or counselor to talk with and vent your issues. If you choose to keep them inside you, the most likely outcome will be feeling worse physically and emotionally. The worse you feel, the more anxious you will become with your claim or appeal.

Take good care of your children and spouse. Those people who have the responsibility of caring for someone else tend to be happier and more productive than those who are alone and without purpose. Your family is the most important thing in the world. A favorable rating decision from the VA is just icing on the cake and will allow you to provide better for your family. But there may be no family if you fail to care for it during this stressful waiting period.

Have a hobby you really enjoy, something to take your mind off all else in your life, especially stressful things. Riding your Harley, fixing up that old Mustang, building RC planes and flying them, playing softball or going bowling each week are all meaningful activities and hobbies that add further meaning to life and, as stated before, take you mind off of your VA case. It's been shown the world over that people with fun hobbies tend to have better and more fulfilling lives, and experience less stress than those who are idle.

Have good friends to talk and share life with. If you have a family, you must nurture them each day, spend meaningful time with them, help them grow and prosper in all ways. If you are single or divorced, then you must develop a good strong bond with other people.

Good things take time and effort, so you should get out of your home and find new friends. Join a book reading group, bowling club, softball team, fishing group, whatever you love doing, and make a great effort to spend time with the people who share your passion and interests. Often we find the best friends in the most unlikely of places, so do make an effort to get out and about and meet new people and experience new things in your life.

Life Goes On

Continue to keep good records of all goings-on and communications with the VA and your case. Have a special storage area for all this correspondence, and keep it well organized so you can find anything you need at a moment's notice.

If you don't have legal representation, keep talking with law firms about getting them to represent you, especially if you have already been denied and are now in the appeal process. There are many attorneys out there who see VA claims as a quick-buck case, so that's why it's important to interview them, even if over the phone.

I spent more than a dozen years talking with attorneys, small law firms and big law firms about my case, and was not happy with any of them so I gave up for a few years. It wasn't until I took a step back and analyzed the actions and behaviors of these attorneys that I realized some are not very good at this and others are great.

Finally, after searching for nearly 10 years, I found an excellent law firm to take on my appeal. They kicked the VA's butt at every turn and even got my effective date of claim moved back nearly 10 years. This law firm did more for me and my case in less than a year than I had done in nearly 20 years on my own or with the "assistance" of veterans service organization representatives.

Funny story: when I told my primary care doc I had just hired a great law firm to handle my appeal, he yelled, "Don't do that! The VA will take care of you and give you what's right!"

Since he was good at taking my blood pressure and heart rate, dispensing a few monthly medications, and monitoring my cholesterol, I didn't say anything, just smiled at him and thanked him for seeing me.

As far as your own case goes, you just have to keep at it until you find a good fit with an attorney or law firm, someone who has an excellent track record against the VA, and who will treat you respectfully.

Do not expect your attorney to be your friend. The best ones out there are rather unfriendly people, but this is not your concern. You want someone who is an expert in the entire VA claims and appeals process, who has an excellent track record, and who is committed to doing an excellent job on your behalf.

The VA claims that attorney's only do marginally better in the appeals process than a veteran on his own. This is a complete lie that is still advertised as truth, because the VA wants veterans to represent themselves in their cases, while the VA is armed with soldiers who are experts in all aspects of the VA claims and appeals process. They have judges and lawyers and clerks who work against the veteran, and the VA wants to keep it this way.

The plain fact is, if you are armed with the same type of ammunition as the VA, i.e. you have a great attorney who believes in your case, you will probably win your case against the VA. And damn the VA's statistics that suggest otherwise.

The best you can do for yourself and your family is to file the best case possible, then let nature take its course while you spend meaningful time with your family, friends and colleagues, doing what you love and sharing it with those you care about. If you're lucky, the VA will come back soon with a favorable decision. If not, keep at it. Good things come to those who are patient . . . and who fight for them. I wish the very best of life for you and your family!

Final Notes on *How To Stay Sane Throughout The Entire Process*:

1. The most important part of the process, once you have filed your claim, is to relax and be patient. There is no substitute for this. If you are disabled to the point of incapacitation, then you must join a group that can support you each day to ensure your mental health is not compromised. If you can exercise, then do so. Just 30 minutes a day is adequate to

keep your mind and body in good shape, but more is always better.

2. If you get antsy, then study the VA claims and appeals process on your own. Ask your attorney for additional resources, do a lot of reading and discovering. Who know? You may come up with a new tactic or strategy that your advisors did not consider.

3. You have been trained to be a cool customer, so learn how to unwind and share your thoughts, ideas, feelings, beliefs with others. There are many groups that gather like-minded people in one place to discuss everything from books to construction projects to parenting. Ask for help when you need it. If you try to do it all on your own, the task may become too daunting.

Q&A

What if I'm a hardass who can't talk to anyone about his feelings?

Call some licensed clinical social workers (LCSW) who do counseling and therapy. I have found these to be the best therapists out there, much more so than psychiatrists and psychologists. A great LCSW who is experienced in working with veterans can be a lifesaver.

It takes time to interview several LCSWs, but the time and effort are worth it. When I was looking for a therapist to talk with about my life and how I needed to make changes,

I went through about 25 different shrinks before someone told me to go see an LCSW. The woman I met I called my "medicine woman," because she was an old soul who was as calm as could be, listened intently, showed great compassion, and had the best suggestions ever. I owe that woman my mental health. It comes down to finding the right fit for you, someone you can trust and feel comfortable with.

Once you find her, loose all the dogs of war from inside your muddy head, then allow your new "medicine woman" to heal you, Brother.

What if my family doesn't care about my VA case?

It's important to have your family's full support. Sit down with them and explain what you are going through, and how important it is to go through the VA disability claims and appeals process with the best possible tools and support.

If they still don't get it, then find a support group that understands the process. There are many veterans' groups out there that offer excellent help and support, so take advantage of one that is a good fit for you.

REFERENCES

The following resources are also available online from the companion website, http://VADisabilityClaimBook.com. They are up to date as of 11 November 2015, so please double-check any references you may use for accuracy.

Should you find any that are inaccurate, please notify the publisher at your earliest convenience:
69@adagiopress.com.

BOOKS

Attig, Chris 2014. *5 Paths to Service Connection*. Satisfied Mind LLC, Dallas, TX.

Attig, Chris. 2014. *Climbing the VA Claims Process: The First Rung on the Ladder of Change in your VA Claim*. Satisfied Mind LLC, Dallas, TX.

Attig, Chris. 2014. *Take Back The Power: How to Get Your VA C-File. How To Get Your VA C&P Exam.* Satisfied Mind LLC, Dallas, TX.

Attig, Chris. 2014. *The Secret to Proving Your VA Claim: A Guide to 5-Star Evidence.* Satisfied Mind LLC, Dallas, TX.

Attig, Chris. 2014. *10 Cases Every Veteran Should Know: Case Law Series #1.* Satisfied Mind LLC, Dallas, TX.

Garner, William Dean A. 2014. *Who Really Owns Your Gold: How The Jesuits Use Gold Economics To Control Humanity.* Adagio Press, Siesta Key, FL.

Jasper, Margaret. 2011. *Veterans' Rights and Benefits* (Legal Almanac Series). Thomson Reuters, Eagan, MN.

PTSD Compensation and Military Service. 2007. Institute of Medicine and National Research Council of the National Academies. The National Academies Press, Washington, DC.

Roche, John D. 2006. *Claim Denied! How to Appeal a VA Denial of Benefits.* Potomac Books, Washington, DC.

Roche, John D. 2006. *The Veteran's Survival Guide: How to File and Collect on VA Claims*, Second Edition. Potomac Books, Washington, DC.

Schoenhard, Paul M. 2011. ***Veterans Affairs Law***. Carolina Academic Press, Durham, NC.

[Multiple Authors] 2013. ***Navigating Legal Issues for Military Veterans: Leading Lawyers On Arguing Disability, Pension, and Other Claims Before the VA.*** Thomson Reuters/ Aspatore, Eagan, MN.

[Multiple Authors] 2008. ***The Changing Landscape of Veterans Affairs: Government Officials on Educating Veterans on Entitled Benefits, Protecting Veterans' Rights, and Initiating Needed Reform.*** Thomson Reuters/Aspatore, Eagan, Minnesota.

[Multiple Editors] 2013. ***Federal Veterans Laws, Rules and Regulations.*** Matthew Bender and Company, Inc., a member of the Lexis-Nexus Group. Charlottesville, VA.

[Multiple Editors] 2013. ***Veterans' Benefits Manual, 2013 Edition.*** Lexis-Nexus, Charlottesville, VA.

Department of Veterans Affairs. 2013. ***Federal Benefits for Veterans, Dependents and Survivors.*** Department of Veterans Affairs: Government Printing Office, Washington, DC.

REPORTS

Coburn, Tom. 24 June 2014. ***Death, Delay and Dismay at the VA: Friendly Fire.*** A Congressional Oversight Report, Washington, DC: Government Printing Office.

ONLINE RESOURCES

VIDEO: How to Get a DoD Self-Service (DS) Logon for eBenefits: https://www.youtube.com/watch?v=QojXqc_TwUk

VIDEO: Step-by-Step Filing of an Electronic Fully Developed Claim (FDC) on eBenefits: https://www.youtube.com/watch?v=RSzX029_ohA&feature=youtu.be

Federal Benefits for Veterans, Dependents and Survivors: http://www.va.gov/opa/publications/benefits_book/2013_Federal_Benefits_for_Veterans_English.pdf

Official VA Search and Download of Complete Lists of Accredited Attorneys, Claims Agents, or VSO Representatives in Excel: http://www.va.gov/ogc/apps/accreditation/index.asp

Search Recognized VSOs: (Questions concerning accreditation of individuals, recognition of organizations, or agents' and attorneys' fees may be sent to ogcaccreditationmailbox@va.gov.): http://www.va.gov/ogc/apps/accreditation/index.asp

Official VA Listing of VSOs: http://www.va.gov/vso/VSO-Directory_2013-2014.pdf

VA Forms, accessible online for reading and downloading: http://www.va.gov/vaforms/

Disability Benefits Questionnaires: http://benefits.va.gov/disabilityexams/

Various types of compensation claims available to apply for: http://www.benefits.va.gov/compensation/types-claims.asp

VA Form 21-526 Veterans Application for Compensation and Pension: http://www.vba.va.gov/pubs/forms/vba-21-526-are.pdf

VA Statement in Support of Claim: http://www.vba.va.gov/pubs/forms/vba-21-4138-are.pdf

VA steps in the compensation claims process: http://www.benefits.va.gov/compensation/process.asp

How to appeal a VA disability claim: http://www.bva.va.gov/docs/Pamphlets/010202A.pdf

Transitioning from the military: https://www.dodtap.mil/

Predischarge claims information:

http://www.benefits.va.gov/predischarge/index.asp

http://www.benefits.va.gov/PREDISCHARGE/claims-pre-discharge-benefits-delivery-at-discharge.asp

http://www.benefits.va.gov/PREDISCHARGE/

disability-exams.asp

Filing a Fully Developed Claim:

http://www.benefits.va.gov/compensation/#slide3

VIDEO: http://www.youtube.com/watch?v=RSzX029_ohA&feature=youtu.be

How To Appeal a Board of Veterans' Appeals Decision: http://www.uscourts.cavc.gov/appeal.php

US Court of Appeals for Veterans Claims: http://www.uscourts.cavc.gov/about.php

US Court of Appeals for Veterans Claims Rules of Practice and Procedure: http://www.uscourts.cavc.gov/rules_of_practice.php

List of court forms for the US Court of Appeals for Veterans Claims: http://www.uscourts.cavc.gov/forms_fees.php

US Court of Appeals for Federal Circuit: Guide For Overview of the VA Disability Claims Process: https://vetadvocates.org/veterans-help/when-to-hire-an-attorney/claims-process/

US Court of Appeals for Federal Circuit: Pro Se Petitioners and Appellants: http://www.cafc.uscourts.gov/images/stories/rules-of-practice/pro_se_updated_2-11-2014.pdf

Veterans Service-Connected Disability Compensation from DisabilitySecrets.com: http://www.disabilitysecrets.com/topics/veterans-service-connected-disability-compensation

Filing for VA Disability Benefits: http://www.disabilitysecrets.com/resources/disability/veterans-disability/filing.htm

Veterans Guide to VA Benefits Online book chapters: http://helpdesk.vetsfirst.org/index.php?pg=kb.book&id=76

Military Separation Guide: http://www.vetsfirst.org/military-separation-guide/

Veterans Benefits Network: http://www.familyofavet.com/veterans_benefits_network.html

What to do and NOT to do when filing a VA claim: http://www.familyofavet.com/va_claim_what_to_do.html

Help with your VA claims: http://www.mrfa.org/VA.Claim.htm

Veterans' blog with articles and statistics about the VA: http://veteransforcommonsense.org/

Information on VA malpractice: http://vaislying.com/2014/06/24/va-pays-one-billion-in-malpractice/

Find a VA-accredited attorney: https://vetadvocates.org/welcome/find-an-attorney/

Website by former trial attorney about VA malfeasance and malpractice: http://www.va-lies.com/

National Organization of Veterans' Advocates, Inc. providing training for those who represent America's veterans: https://vetadvocates.org/

National Organization of Veterans' Advocates, Inc.'s resources for Vets: https://vetadvocates.org/resources/

The Veterans Consortium Pro Bono Program Providing Representation to Veterans at the U.S. Court of Appeals for Veterans Claims: http://www.vetsprobono.org/

The Veterans Consortium Pro Bono Program brochure: http://www.vetsprobono.org/wp-content/uploads/2011/05/Veterans-Pro-Bono-Brochure-2014.pdf

USEFUL VA CONTACT INFORMATION

Bereavement Counseling: 1-202-461-6530
Civilian Health and Medical Program (CHAMPVA): 800-733-8387
Caregiver Support: 855-260-3274
Debt Management Center: 800-827-0648
Education: 888-442-4551
Federal Recovery Coordination Program: 877-732-4456
Foreign Medical Program: 888-820-1756
Headstones and Markers: 800-697-6947
Healthcare: 877-222-8387
Homeless Veterans: 877-424-3838
Home Loans: 888-827-3702
Life Insurance: 800-669-8477
National Cemetery Scheduling Office: 800-535-1117
Pension Management Center: 877-294-6380
Presidential Memorial Certificate Program: 202-565-4964
Special Health Issues: 800-749-8387
Telecommunication Device for the Deaf: 800-829-4833
VA Benefits: 800-827-1000
VA Combat Call Center: 877-927-8387
VA Records Management Center: 888-533-4558
Veterans Crisis Line: 800-273-8255
Women Veterans: 877-222-8387

Burial and Memorial Benefits: cem.va.gov
Caregiver Support: caregiver.va.gov
CHAMPVA: va.gov/hac/forbeneficiaries/forbeneficiaries.asp

eBenefits: ebenefits.va.gov
Education Benefits: gibill.va.gov
Environmental Exposures: publichealth.va.gov/exposures
Healthcare Eligibility: va.gov/healthbenefits
Homeless Veterans: va.gov/homeless
Home Loan Guaranty: homeloans.va.gov
Life Insurance: insurance.va.gov
Memorial Certificate Program: cem.va.gov/pmc.asp
Mental Health: mentalhealth.va.gov
My HealtheVet: myhealth.va.gov
National Resource Directory: nrd.gov
Prosthetics: prosthetics.va.gov
Records: archives.gov/st-louis/military-personnel
Returning Servicemembers: oefoif.va.gov
State Departments of Veterans Affairs: va.gov/statedva.htm
Women Veterans: womenshealth.va.gov
VA Vet Centers: vetcenter.va.gov
VA Home Page: va.gov
VA Benefit Payment Rates: vba.va.gov/bln/21/rates
VA Forms: va.gov/vaform
Vocational Rehabilitation and Employment: vetsuccess.gov

PURCHASE OUR BOOKS

Our books can be purchased on
Amazon stores worldwide
AdagioPress.com
WilliamDeanAGarner.com
RioRamirez.com
SeanMaclarenBooks.com
VADisabilityClaimBook.com
BarnesandNoble.com and
Apple iTunes Bookstore

Please enjoy browsing our selection. . . .

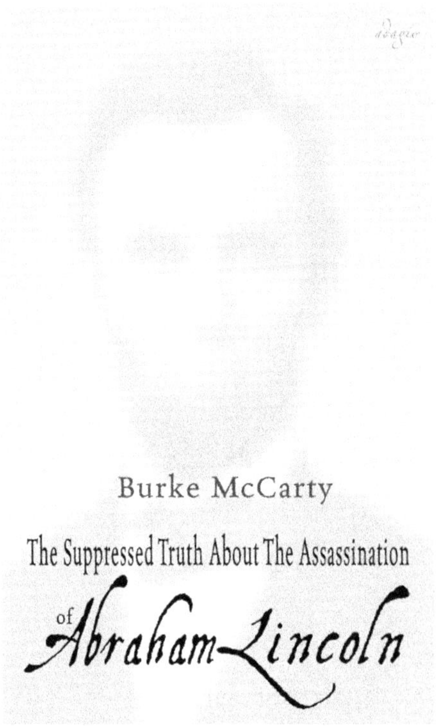

The Suppressed Truth About the Assassination of Abraham Lincoln

Ex-Catholic Burke McCarty spent years researching the details surrounding the murder of President Abraham Lincoln, who was one of the few American politicians who openly acknowledged that the Jesuits were a menace to our society, but he felt powerless to do anything about the threat.

This hidden gem should be read by every person who calls himself or herself an American, as it uncovers an ongoing sinister plot to overthrow the liberties of our beloved nation and her people.

You owe it to yourself to read the well-carved thoughts of this brave woman who risked her own life to present the facts that most others continue to ignore, even 150 years after the murder of President Lincoln.

Paperback available from Amazon.com and other retail outlets

eBook available from WilliamDeanAGarner.com and AdagioPress.com

THE PRINCE

Machiavelli's ***The Prince*** has become a classic over the centuries since it first appeared around 1510, not because of its elegance or style but because of its subversive content about the true nature of power. Mainstream historians and academics have labelled it a "political treatise," but this is only a small part of the picture.

The Prince isn't just for princes who thirst for, or are forcibly thrown into, advancement.

It is a raw and bloody field manual for upper- and mid-level managers on predatorial ethics and power: what it is, how to obtain it, and what to do with it once you have found, stumbled across, or been granted it.

Paperback available from Amazon.com and other retail outlets

eBook available from WilliamDeanAGarner.com and AdagioPress.com

ROMANIC DEPRESSION
How the Jesuits Designed, Built and Destroyed America

Sean Mclaren has carefully researched and written the two sequels to ***Who Really Owns Your Gold***, which was an introductory historical perspective about the Jesuits and their malevolent actions and behaviors over the past 100-plus years in America. In this ground-breaking volume, he analyzes and examines 40 sectors of American society, and demonstrate how the Jesuits have designed and built, and manipulated and corrupted each one, then marketed and advertised something decidedly contrary.

The book's Reference section contains more than 200 books about the Jesuits. If you take the time to read even a few of them, your heart, mind and soul will expand immensely, and you will begin to understand what others have known for centuries: this brood of snakes and vipers has done, and continues to do, great harm to humanity. . . .

Paperback available from Amazon.com and other retail outlets

eBook available from WilliamDeanAGarner.com, SeanMaclarenBooks.com and AdagioPress.com

ARCANUM
A critical analysis of the original 36 sermons of Jmmanuel, the man known to the world as Jesus Christ

ARCANUM by Sean Maclaren is one of two sequels to *Who Really Owns Your Gold*, which was an introductory historical perspective about the Jesuits and their malevolent actions and behaviors over the past 100-plus years in America.

The 410-page sequel is a highly detailed and provocative two-part essay:

Part One is an unsparing, meticulous and diligent analysis and evaluation of each of the original 36 sermons of Jmmanuel Sananda, the half-extraterrestrial/half-human known to the world as Jesus Christ.

Part Two is an actual full English translation and new edit (for clarity and readability) of the 36 extant sermons of Jmmanuel Sananda, the man known to the world as Jesus Christ.

Paperback available from Amazon.com and other retail outlets

eBook available from WilliamDeanAGarner.com and AdagioPress.com

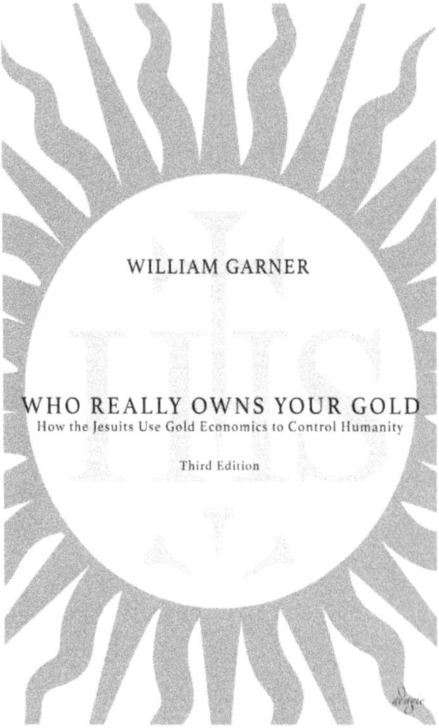

***Who Really Owns Your Gold How The Jesuits Use Gold Economics To Control Humanity*, Third Edition**

The power that controls your gold, your assets and your life is a dynastic group of men in Rome, and it's not the Vatican. They control every government on the planet and, using celestiophysics, manipulate to their advantage all actions and behaviors in law, politics, economics and finance, business, law enforcement, military and defense affairs, science and high-tech, entertainment, medicine and healthcare, education, etc.

New York Times bestselling ghostwriter and editor William Dean A. Garner takes you on a journey into a labyrinth where up is down, black is white, yes is no . . . and nothing is what it seems.

This revelation is for everyone, not just those who "own" gold or precious metals.

Paperback available from Amazon.com and other retail outlets

eBook available from WilliamDeanAGarner.com and AdagioPress.com

Sun Tzu *The Art of War* *Ancient Wisdom . . . Modern Twist*

New York Times bestselling author Dalton Fury has this to say about William Dean A. Garner's updated version of *The Art of War*: "Dean Garner's version of *The Art of War* confirms for us that for the past 2,000 years the fundamental principles of special operations in battle have not only remained true, but they apply equally to today's boardrooms and bedrooms. When on the hunt or holding ground, success can only be had by the precise application of disguise, deception and diversion, and a genuine appreciation for angles, inches, and seconds. Ranger Garner masterfully shows us how."

Paperback available from Amazon.com and other retail outlets

eBook available from WilliamDeanAGarner.com and AdagioPress.com

How To Write Your First Book
A Simple & Practical Method
For Anyone Who Can Tell a Story

This gem is much more than just a book about writing. It reveals metaphysically how our subconscious functions during the creative process to produce the finished product, and how we grow spiritually as this process evolves before us to create our first book.

Garner employs a simple, step-by-step method we have used all our lives, and includes easy-to-follow examples and exercises, plus anecdotes from his work as a ghostwriter/editor on some very sexy novels and books.

Paperback available from Amazon.com and other retail outlets
eBook available from AdagioPress.com

CPSIA information can be obtained
at www.ICGtesting.com
Printed in the USA
LVHW03s0319150618
580860LV00003B/294/P

9 780996 767729